OTHER TITLES OF INTEREST

An Introduction to Networks for PC and Mac Users

by
Daniel, Christine
and
Owen Bishop

BERNARD BABANI (publishing) LTD
THE GRAMPIANS
SHEPHERDS BUSH ROAD
LONDON W6 7NF
ENGLAND

PLEASE NOTE

Although every care has been taken with the production of this book to ensure that any projects, designs, modifications and/or programs, etc., contained herewith, operate in a correct and safe manner and also that any components specified are normally available in Great Britain, the Publisher and Author(s) do not accept responsibility in any way for the failure (including fault in design) of any project, design, modification or program to work correctly or to cause damage to any equipment that it may be connected to or used in conjunction with, or in respect of any other damage or injury that may be so caused, nor do the Publishers accept responsibility in any way for the failure to obtain specified components.

Notice is also given that if equipment that is still under warranty is modified in any way or used or connected with home-built equipment then that warranty may be void.

© 1995 BERNARD BABANI (publishing) LTD

First Published - April 1995

British Library Cataloguing in Publication Data:

Bishop, D.
  Introduction to Networks for PC and MAC Users
  I. Title
  004.616

  ISBN 0 85934 373 1

Printed and Bound in Great Britain by Cox & Wyman Ltd, Reading

PREFACE

This book is for all PC and Macintosh users who would like to know more about networks, what they are, and what they can offer. No prior knowledge of networks is assumed.

In Chapter 1, various different types of networks are outlined: Local Area Networks, Wide Area Networks, Bulletin Board Systems and the Internet. Both commercial and non-commercial uses of networks are highlighted. Chapter 2 describes what a Local Area Network is, what it can do for you, and how to use it. Chapter 3 explains the hardware and software involved in the operation of a Local Area Network. In Chapter 4, you will learn how to use other computers remotely on your Local Area Network or via the Internet. Also, find out how File Transfer Protocol may be used to get useful programs from archives around the world. Chapter 5 introduces and explains the world of electronic mail (or e-mail). Not only can you send messages, programs and other data around the world, in seconds, you can now even send faxes. Chapter 6 introduces Network News, not just a world-wide conferencing system, but a global community. Catch a glimpse of the 'Information Superhighway' in Chapter 7, which describes how to access Internet information servers using Archie, WAIS, Gopher and World Wide Web. The wealth of information available at your fingertips will amaze you, but is only a taste of what is yet to come!

A comprehensive glossary at the end of this book defines every technical term used, and means that you will never be bamboozled by 'netspeak' again!

D., C. & O. Bishop

ABOUT THE AUTHORS

Daniel Bishop has written over 30 articles for computer magazines. Daniel and Christine have gained considerable experience in using computer networks at various universities in the UK and New Zealand. Owen Bishop is well known as a contributor to popular computing and electronics magazines and is author of over 60 books, mostly in computing and electronics.

ACKNOWLEDGEMENTS

The authors would like to thank Novell UK Ltd for providing information on their network products. The University of Edinburgh and Victoria University of Wellington are also thanked for providing computing facilities during the writing of this book.

TRADEMARKS

CONTENTS

Chapter 1

WHAT IS A NETWORK?

In this chapter we will introduce you to the fundamental concepts of computers and computer networks. To be able to understand how present-day networks function, we will firstly look at networks and computers from a historical perspective. The construction of current networks owes a great legacy to the past. There are now four broad categories of networks, with which most people will come into contact. These are LANs (Local Area Networks), WANs (Wide Area Networks), BBSs (Bulletin Board Systems), and the Internet. These categories are not always mutually exclusive, so for example, a network may be both a BBS and part of the Internet, or, a network may be a LAN, but also part of a WAN. Although there are many grey areas, these categories of networks do have some defining characteristics, which are outlined in this chapter.

LANs are found in most types of organisations, such as schools, universities, government departments and both small and large businesses. The different kinds of LAN are described in this chapter. WANs are normally used only by large organisations, particularly big commercial organisations, for which it is important to have a network that can cover a large geographical area and handle large amounts of data very rapidly. Both the technology involved, and the commercial applications of WANs are discussed in this chapter. BBSs also provide a wealth of information for commercial customers, as well as the computer hobbyist at home. BBSs are also particularly useful for those who wish to use networks by phone. The Internet is the much vaunted forerunner of the so-called 'Information Superhighway', and has something for everyone. It provides a common link between LANs, WANs and BBSs, and so is something that nearly every network user will come across. The history of the Internet, what it is, what it provides and how to connect to it, are all described in the last part of this chapter.

Computers and Networks

During the 1950's, 60's and 70's, the physical size of computers was very much greater than today. In those days, electronic circuitry was much bulkier, since originally valves, and later transistors were the main components. Some of these computers could occupy up to several rooms of a building, and were called 'mainframes', whilst the smaller ones, called 'minicomputers', were still large by present standards. Access to these computers was commonly through a 'terminal', which consisted of a keyboard and monitor screen only. Several terminals would be wired into the main computer, allowing a number of users to share the computer's resources (Figure 1.1).

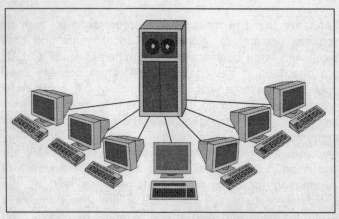

Figure 1.1 Connection of terminals to a mainframe computer.

Superficially, these terminals were similar to modern PCs and Macintoshes. However, they differed in that they could not function on their own, had no computing power of their own, and were thus known as 'dumb' terminals. These mainframes and their terminals were the forerunners of modern computer networks.

With the advent of the microprocessor, computers became much smaller and faster. Increasing miniaturisation and better design of microprocessors, computer memory chips and electronic circuit boards, eventually culminated in the creation of the microcomputer, a machine much more powerful than the original mainframes, but small enough to rest comfortably on a desktop. The PC and the Macintosh are the two best-selling microcomputers of the 1980's and 90's. In addition to PCs and Macintoshes, there are a plethora of other computers now available, which range from hand-held and pocket computers to mainframes, all of which are orders of magnitude more powerful than the mainframes and minicomputers of the 1950's, 60's and 70's.

A PC or Macintosh that is connected to nothing but the power supply, and perhaps a printer or scanner, will satisfy the computing needs of many people. Such a computer is often referred to as a 'stand-alone' machine, and is perfectly adequate for such activities as word-processing, graphical work, and playing games. However, the ability to connect with other computers can increase the power and usefulness of a computer several fold.

Today, millions of computers in academic institutions, businesses and the home are linked to one another, by special electrical cables, via the telephone system, or via satellite and radio links. Such connected groups of computers are known as 'networks'. A network may consist of just a handful of computers in one room or office, or may comprise thousands of computers around the world. A network allows the user to use printers, disk drives, scanners and other devices that are not actually attached to the user's computer. Furthermore, a network allows the user to access and run programs on other computers, transfer files and programs from place to place, look up information in public and private databases, and to communicate with other network users, using text, pictures and even sound.

Meanwhile, the 'dumb' terminals are not quite extinct, although they may be soon, since they can cost as much, or more than a PC or Macintosh, either of which can perform the same job. They are still used with some mainframes, and are sometimes used in networks. For example, terminals are often used in Unix workstation-based networks. So, if you see a room full of monitors and keyboards in a company or in a university department, do not assume that they are all separate computers. They may well only be terminals! However, through them it is likely that you can access a network, and hence, be able to use facilities and access data, on other computers.

Local Area Networks (LANs)
The simplest sort of network is the Local Area Network, or LAN. Computers in a LAN are always connected via special electrical cables, one of the most popular varieties being Ethernet. Although these cables allow fast communication between the computers on the LAN, and allow a considerable volume of electronic data to be transmitted, their capacity is not limitless. In practice, a LAN rarely has more than a few hundred computers connected, and seldom extends beyond a few adjacent buildings.

LANs exist in both commercial and non-commercial environments, and are equally useful in both. In both cases, a typical LAN will consist of a few dozen PCs or Macintoshes, together with some other devices, such as a printer or two, a scanner, and perhaps a CD-ROM. In more extreme cases, a LAN may comprise just two or three computers in one room, or several hundred in a large office, school or university. Most LANs are operated with hardware and software from the major manufacturers, such as Novell, Microsoft, IBM and Apple.

A LAN can be used to perform a variety of tasks. Data can be transferred from one machine to another, without needing to carry floppy disks about. LAN users can share data and programs lodged on different machines. All users can share peripheral devices such as printers, scanners, extra disk drives and tape drives, etc. Users can also send messages and electronic mail (known as 'e-mail') to other users of the LAN. Such messages are transmitted in a fraction of a second, and are immediately available to the recipient who is logged-in to the LAN, or are stored until he or she next logs-in to the LAN.

In the simplest form of LAN, all of the computers operate on the 'peer-to-peer principle', i.e. all of the computers (and users) in the LAN share disk drives, printers and possibly other peripheral devices too (Figure 1.2). No computer is dedicated to running the LAN, and each user can control the level of access other users have to their computer and its connected devices, i.e. their computer's resources. Resources may include disk drives, directories and files, as well as hardware devices such as printers. The amount of control any user has, depends on which software is being used to run the peer-to-peer LAN, but typically, the LAN user can limit access to particular users, or restrict other users to reading, but not editing or deleting certain files. He or she may even be able to set up certain files so that they are 'invisible' to other LAN users, if total privacy is important.

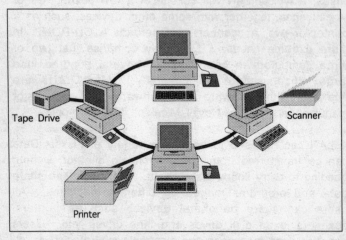

Tape Drive

Scanner

Printer

Figure 1.2 A typical peer-to-peer LAN configuration.

In larger LANs, it is usually sensible to have one computer that is dedicated to administering the LAN and the peripherals attached to the LAN (such as printers, scanners, disk drives, etc.). This computer is called the 'file server', or simply the 'server', and the other computers on the LAN are called 'clients' (Figure 1.3). Compared to the other computers on the LAN, the server should be relatively powerful, running special server software, and have large disk drives and fast printers attached, so that it can adequately deal with the demands of all the LAN users, simultaneously, if needs be. A server-based LAN should be set up and maintained by a system manager or administrator (Chapter 2), and, as long as everything is running smoothly, it should be possible to leave the server running unattended for days, weeks or even longer.

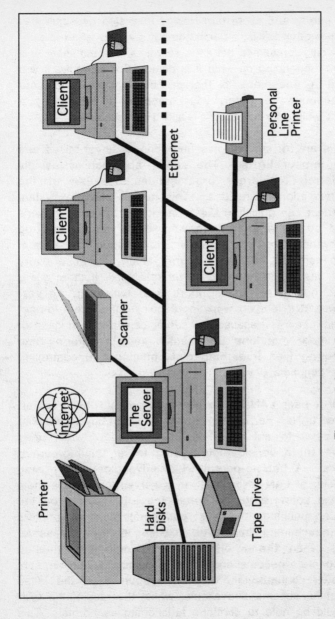

Figure 1.3 A typical server-based LAN configuration.

The server and client terminology may also be applied to peer-to-peer LANs. Each computer on a peer-to-peer LAN can sometimes act as a server, and sometimes as a client, depending on what it is doing. For example, if you send a document to the printer connected to your neighbour's computer, your computer is acting as a client, while your neighbour's is acting as a server.

There are, of course, pros and cons to server-based and peer-to-peer LANs. The server approach is usually preferred by larger organisations because of the centralisation it provides. This means that the system manager can quickly make a back-up copy of the server's hard disks, rather than having to individually back-up every computer on the LAN. In addition, the system manager can maintain security easily, because every user has to log-in to the server machine. If there are a large number of users (more than ten, say), server-based LANs tend to work more quickly than peer-to-peer LANs. This is because the server can take over most of the more mundane LAN tasks, such as storing and retrieving files from hard disk, printing and controlling other peripheral devices.

Peer-to-peer LANs have some advantages over server-based LANs. For example, the expense of buying an extra computer to act as a server is avoided, which may represent a considerable saving for a small group of users. A peer-to-peer LAN is advantageous for easy sharing of LAN resources. In a server-based LAN, most of the software that operates the LAN resides on the server machine, and most peripherals such as printers are attached to the server. Consequently, if the server fails, then the whole LAN fails and the attached peripherals become unavailable. In contrast, in a peer-to-peer configuration, only the resources on the failed machine become unavailable, whilst the rest of the LAN should be able to continue functioning as normal. This

8

said, peer-to-peer LANs require some degree of co-operation between users. For example, if someone else is using a program on your computer remotely from their computer, they will not be pleased if you switch your computer off and go home! This is unlikely to happen in server-based LANs since the server is normally left running all the time.

In general, a peer-to-peer LAN is most suitable for small networks, (where the number of users is not more than about five) otherwise a server-based LAN is more appropriate.

Wide Area Networks (WANs)

A Wide Area Network, or WAN is, as its name suggests, a network that covers a large geographical area such as a city, a country or even the globe. A WAN may comprise several LANs, a number of individual computers, or a mixture of both. WANs are connected by a variety of means, as opposed to LANs which use only dedicated electrical cables. WAN connections are commonly provided by specialist telecommunication companies. Types of connections include special high-capacity, high-speed cables suitable for long distances (optical fibre cables are particularly suitable for this purpose), telephone networks, radio and satellite links. Because of the complexity and expense of setting them up, most WANs are operated in the commercial environment.

Commercial telecommunications companies that provide WAN connections include BT, Mercury, AT&T, France Telecom, and many others. There are a number of options, such as X.25, ISDN, and ATM amongst others, which are described below. The most suitable option for a particular WAN depends upon the quantity, speed and frequency of data to be transmitted. Picking the wrong kind of WAN for the job can lead to unnecessarily high operational costs.

The X.25 network system is particularly suited for larger networks and is designed to receive data in packets, which may be sent at any time across the network. This network is therefore useful for data transmission, but not interactive use of software over the network. X.25 networks commonly use existing PSTN (Public Switched Telephone Network) lines to carry data. A number of companies offer private X.25-based networks for businesses. For example, within the UK, companies such as Imminus (Midland Network Services) provide WAN network services and Internet access for business customers. They use the X.25 system for moving information around the country.

The Paknet system also uses X.25, but it communicates by radio transmissions rather than telephone lines. Thus Paknet is particularly useful for business users who are more often out of the office than in. It has already found applications within security companies.

ISDN (Integrated Services Digital Network) is another option for WAN communication. This is a high-speed private communications link, which is widely used for access to databases in the UK and elsewhere. ISDN is most appropriate if the requirement of the WAN is to access remote computer sites regularly, but only for short periods of time.

In the near future, more and more WANs will be using the ATM (Asynchronous Transfer Mode) system, rather than systems such as X.25. This is a relatively new system for sending information around global networks. The information sent is electronically pre-packaged and addressed before sending, using a standard format. ATM is ideally suited to larger WANs, which carry very large quantities of data, such as audio and visual data. One of the pioneers of ATM, Stratacom has provided a number of ATM networks for large clients such as BT and Mercury.

X.500 is a system used in large networks such as WANs. It was developed by the CCITT (Comite Consultatif International Telegraphique et Telephonique). It is specifically designed for administering very large databases which are distributed over a number of computers in a network. X.500 provides network users with rapid access to databases, and is often used by large organisations such as companies and universities to create databases of personnel details, such as electronic mail addresses, phone numbers and postal addresses. Such databases are sometimes called 'white pages directories'.

Airlines and travel agents around the World use SITA, a world-wide airline communications network represerting most of the leading airlines. Travel agents use computer reservation systems such as Galileo, Sabre and Amadeus, which are all connected through SITA. One of the largest international commercial networks has been developed by British Airways and Qantas. They are working towards total integration of their airline databases, using the BABS system (British Airways Booking System), which is IBM and TPS-based (Transaction Processing System). This system will allow connection between SITA, British Airways and Qantas PCs world-wide.

Financial companies and news services are now heavily reliant on rapid transfer of large volumes of data world-wide, and many of these companies have designed and developed their own WANs. For example, the international news agency, Reuters uses its own network IDN (International Data Network) to collate information from a very wide variety of sources.

Bulletin Board Systems (BBSs)

Originally, a BBS was a computer network that provided users with the ability to contribute news and messages. It allowed all other users to read these contributions, and, if they wished, respond to them. Some BBSs are non-commercial and can be reached via the Internet, which is described below. One such service is Usenet, which provides the popular Network News service, described in Chapter 6. However, there are now a large number of commercial BBSs that can be reached by phone using a modem, which provide users with a whole variety of services. BBSs usually contain large amounts of information, such as news, weather reports, financial information, travel information, as well as computer data, programs and other files. One of the big attractions for many BBS subscribers is the availability of vast numbers of cheap or free computer programs, including games, utilities, and business software. BBSs may offer other facilities such as shopping. They are interactive, which means users can contribute to what is available on the BBS, communicate with other BBS users and users of the Internet. As well as sending messages, it is often possible to 'chat' in real-time to other users, using your keyboard rather than the phone. Clearly, this has advantages when the other users are far away, saving long distance phone charges. The services are paid for by subscription charges, on-line charges and advertising revenue.

There is a huge number of commercial BBSs world-wide, over 100,000 in the USA, and a growing number in the UK, which include Auntie, CityScape, CIX (Compulink Information Exchange), CompuServe, Connect, Demon Internet, EUnet, eWorld, Frontier Internet Service, The Microsoft Network, PIPEX, and The Direct Connection.

BBS adverts are to be found in almost all computer magazines. To join, you will need to phone or write to the relevant organisation, telling them which type of computer you are using and the services you are most interested in. You will have to pay to join the bulletin board; the payment may be in the form of a registration charge, and/or a monthly or annual subscription charge. A few bulletin boards are totally free, several offer some services free, while many offer a free introductory period or free demonstration. Check the computer magazines for special offers. It is well worth trying before you buy, to see what you get for your money.

If you are going to connect your computer to the bulletin board via a modem, you will need to buy the modem and software to drive the modem (Figure 1.4). The bulletin board company should be able to supply you with the necessary hardware and software, or at least advise you where you might be able to get them from. You will also have to pay telephone charges while connected to the BBS. Check with the bulletin board company to see whether you will have to pay local rates, or long-distance rates, and whether it depends on the day and time of day. You are likely to pay less for connection if you live close to a large city, where access phone numbers are generally provided for bulletin board customers.

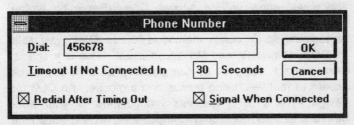

Figure 1.4 Using Windows to make a modem connection.

If you connect to the bulletin board via your LAN and the Internet, you won't have to pay phone charges, but you may well have to pay a charge to the bulletin board vendor whilst you are on-line, i.e. connected to their computer.

There are a wide variety of services available on bulletin boards, but check with the various companies as some are more likely to suit your interests and needs than others. Some BBSs are aimed at PC users, some at Macintosh users, and some are meant for both.

To illustrate how a typical BBS works, we will look at one of the larger ones, CompuServe, as an example. CompuServe was started in 1979 and currently has over 1.6 million members around the world. It is available 24 hours a day, every day of the year. It offers over 1,700 different products and services, and over 350,000 files are available for downloading. In addition, over 700 computer companies provide hardware and software support through this system.

CompuServe can be accessed from your computer by using a terminal program, or using the CompuServe *Information Manager (CIM)*, or using an off-line reader (OLR). There are a number of basic terminal programs around, such as Microsoft *Windows* Terminal program. These will allow you to access CompuServe by typing commands at a command prompt. Using this method can be tedious, so an easier method is to use *CIM*, available for DOS, *Windows*, and Macintosh users. This is a special user interface designed by CompuServe to allow you quick access to features, using menus and a mouse. An OLR (or navigator) is a utility that lets you do most of your work before and after accessing CompuServe, saving telephone and access charges. There are a number of commercially available OLR programs, such as *WinNav*, a *Windows*-based OLR from CompuServe itself. You must firstly give it instructions about the data you want to access, so that when it logs-in it will be able to perform the operation automatically and log-out quickly. Obviously, you need to know what you want, and therefore you will also need a terminal program, or *CIM* to explore the CompuServe system.

The level of services provided on CompuServe can be basic, extended or premium. These levels provide different facilities and are priced at different rates. Basic services include e-mail, various reference databases, some games, shopping and news, sport and weather information. To gain access to all the databases and conferencing areas, you will need to become an extended or premium user. Payment for services is usually done through a credit card for personal users. Business users can arrange for costs to be invoiced to their company.

There are, of course, many other BBSs, which provide different combinations of facilities and different pricing schemes. Some of the more popular ones include those described below. Contact postal addresses for all the BBSs mentioned are provided in Appendix 2 at the back of this book. Readers may write to these addresses for detailed information on services and prices.

CIX offers a large selection of conference and news facilities, and access to the Internet. Connect is for PC users, gives access to the UseNet system and a library of software to download. The Microsoft Network offers access to Microsoft technical support and many other services such as Internet access. Apple has a BBS called eWorld that provides industry news and technical help for Macintosh users. A recently launched BBS is called Auntie, and is provided by the BBC Networking Club. It is particularly aimed at educational users, and also allows access to the Internet. EUnet is a BBS service for commercial customers only, and provides Internet access as well as other BBS facilities. CityScape, Demon Internet, Frontier Internet Service, The Direct Connection and PIPEX provide modem users with an easy way to get onto the Internet.

The Internet

In addition to LANs, WANs, and BBSs, there are a number of non-commercial networks that are national or global in scale. These networks have developed on a more *ad hoc* basis, often by integration of smaller networks. Mostly they have their roots in academia and government research. Characteristically these networks tend to use a great variety of hardware and software, are not very structured, regulated or controlled, and are mostly open to the public. Because they are less orderly and less regulated, these networks are more easily able to expand and evolve. The largest and best known example is called the 'Internet', which is, in fact, not a single network, but a loose alliance of a huge number of smaller networks.

Networks that are not part of the Internet, such as WANs and BBSs, are sometimes called 'outernets'. However, most of these networks have links to the Internet, known as 'gateways' or 'bridges' (Figure 1.5).

The history of the Internet can be traced back to the establishment of the ARPANET (Advanced Research Projects Agency Network) by the United States Department of Defense in 1969. This network was in operation throughout the 1970's and 80's, and was not finally dismantled until 1990. In the meantime, it spawned many other networks, and was itself divided into the ARPANET and Milnet (an entirely military network) in the early 80's, as the ARPANET became more widely used by American universities. Early experimental networks that were connected to the ARPANET used DARPA technology (the ARPA become DARPA by the addition of 'Defense' at the beginning). The ARPANET and these other fledgling networks became known collectively as the

16

DARPA Internet, which later became known more simply as the 'Internet'.

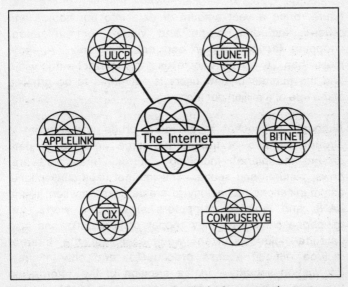

Figure 1.5 The Internet and other networks.

Other networks came into being in the 1970's, such as the UUCP for users of computers running the Unix language (so named because it used the Unix to Unix Copy Program). Another network that came into being at this time was the USENET (User's Network), meant to be used by both universities and commercial organisations. More networks appeared in the 1980's, such as CSNET (Computer Science Network), BITNET (the Because It's There Network, or alternatively, the Because It's Time Network), and the important NSFNET (National Science Foundation Network). The popularity of the NSFNET was one of the reasons why the ARPANET was dismantled. Other networks also appeared elsewhere in the World, such as JANET (Joint Academic Network) in Britain.

The Internet is thought by many to be the forerunner of what is often called the 'Information Superhighway', the conceptual global electronic network that will, in the near future, bring a vast amount of data into our homes and offices, including audio and visual communication, shopping facilities, news and entertainment. Already, more than 20 million people use the Internet world-wide, and the number of new users is estimated to be growing at the rate of a million per month.

Although its mechanics are quite crude, the Internet is already capable of transferring large amounts of data around the planet, including electronic mail, software, news, pictures and sound. The Internet uses conventional communications technology to create links between all the LANs and isolated computers around the world, i.e. telephone cables, be they copper or fibre-optic, and also satellite links. Current weaknesses of the Internet include difficult access procedures, and only minimal information security. In the creation of the 'Information Superhighway' of the future, these two problems will have to be addressed.

The Internet is run by a variety of different companies and academic groups in different countries. For the system to function properly, certain protocols and guidelines must be adhered to, but apart from that there is little in the way of international regulation or control. In essence, the Internet is a very loose collection of connected networks and information providers.

Macintosh and PC users can connect to the Internet by a variety of methods, although in all cases you must be able to access a computer that is directly connected to the Internet, called an Internet 'host' computer. This is commonly done via a LAN or via a modem.

If your PC or Macintosh is part of a LAN which is connected to the Internet, then you can access the Internet through this connection. In this case, your PC or Macintosh will have an Internet address (Chapter 4) and is also an Internet host computer.

If you do not use a LAN, you may still connect to the Internet, if you can connect directly to an Internet host computer. Within a university or another large institution, your computing officer may be able to get your PC or Macintosh directly connected to an Internet host machine, using one of the special network cabling technologies. Again, your computer will then be an Internet host computer.

Alternatively, you may be able to connect to an Internet host over the telephone, by using a modem. This solution may be more convenient if you work from home, or use the Internet just as a hobby. You will also need special software to run your modem, and to allow you to interact with the host computer. Depending on the type of connection and the type of software that you use, your computer may simply act as a terminal to the Internet host machine, or your computer may be transformed into a full Internet host itself. You can get either kind of connection from a BBS, although you will have to pay for their services. If you can connect to a local university or local government council Internet host instead, it will almost certainly be cheaper. In some countries, such as New Zealand, free Internet access is provided by the local government council, and in some parts of the US, there are free public networks (called Freenets) which provide Internet access.

Chapter 2

YOUR LOCAL AREA NETWORK

Many people's first experience of using a network will be of using a LAN (Local Area Network). LANs are now common in universities, schools, government departments and businesses. It becomes increasingly likely that the PC or Macintosh that you use at work every day is connected to a LAN, even though you may not be aware of this! A LAN can increase the usefulness of your computer in many ways, and you owe it to yourself to find out how to get the most from your LAN. This chapter tells you how.

Firstly we show you how to connect to your LAN from your computer, and then show you what you can (and cannot!) do. Topics covered include the server computer, which is the computer that lies at the heart of many LANs. We also discuss the various disk drives that may be available to you, where files are kept on these disk drives, and who may use them. Most LANs will have at least one printer attached, and possibly several, which you may be able to use from your PC or Macintosh. This chapter explains how to access your LAN printers. Also, you will learn how to exchange messages and files with other people on your LAN. When you start using a LAN, you will soon get to know the system manager. This chapter describes what a system manager does, and how to keep on the right side of your system manager. Two issues which are of particular importance to both you as a user and the system manager are the security of the network, and the avoidance of computer viruses, topics that are discussed at the end of this chapter.

Logging-In

If you are not sure whether your PC or Macintosh is connected to a LAN or not, look at the back of your computer. If you are connected, there will be a cable plugged into the back of your computer, (other than the power cable) which leads to a special wall socket, a special network junction box, or another computer (the hardware required for a LAN is described in Chapter 3). It is not enough just to have the physical connections, though. You must also have the appropriate network software correctly installed and configured on your computer, and the LAN itself must be active (the software required for a LAN is also described in Chapter 3). If you do not have the right hardware, or software, or the network is inactive, you will not be able to connect to the network.

Connecting to the network is often called 'logging-in', or 'logging-on', and the procedure is described below. If your computer is not connected to the LAN, and you believe it should be, or you experience problems logging-in, then you should contact your LAN system manager for help. They should be able to set up your computer with the required hardware and software so that you can use the LAN.

If your PC or Macintosh is properly connected to a LAN, there are at least three possible ways in which your computer may behave when you switch it on, depending on how your LAN and your computer have been configured. Firstly, you may have to 'log-in' to the LAN, before you can carry on. Secondly, your computer may be set up so that you do not have to log-in to the LAN, before you can carry on, but you may have to log-in if you wish to use any of the LAN facilities. Lastly, your computer may automatically log-in for you, in which case you will have access to the LAN immediately, with the minimum of fuss.

21

On a Macintosh, logging-in is usually achieved by selecting the LAN from the Chooser pull-down menu. On a PC it depends on how your system is set up, but normally you will have to select and run a special log-in program, either through DOS or *Windows*.

In order to log-in you must do two things. Firstly, when prompted, you must type in your 'user name' (sometimes called a 'user ID'). Secondly, you must type in your 'password' (Figure 2.1). Your user name tells the LAN who you are, what privileges you have on the LAN, what devices you have access to and what files on the server belong to you.

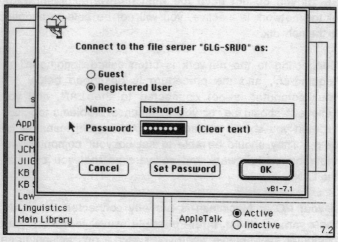

Figure 2.1 Logging-in to the server on a Macintosh.

Your presence on the network can be detected by the LAN system manager and your activity may be monitored, for example, if you are using a printer. Your user name must be unique on the LAN, otherwise the LAN would not be able to distinguish between users. So, even if there are two people with the name Joe Bloggs using the LAN, they must have different user names. In this example, there are several obvious alternatives, such as JOE, BLOGGS, JBloggs, BloggsJ, Bloggs1, Bloggs2, JB, etc. The user name must be typed correctly, otherwise the LAN will not recognise it. If you make an error before pressing the *return* or *enter* key you can use the *backspace* and *delete* keys to correct your error. If you forget your user name, your system manager will be able to remind you, since he or she can access a list of all user names registered on the LAN.

Once you have entered your user name during log-in, you will usually have to enter your password. A password identifies you as the real owner of the user name, since nobody else should know your password except you. When you first get your user name, your system manager may know your password, but you must change it immediately for reasons of network security, as described later in this chapter. If you forget your password, don't worry! Simply ask your system manager to give you a new one.

When you type in your password at log-in time, the characters that you type will not appear on the screen, or may appear on the screen as asterisks or dots. This is for security, so that someone looking over your shoulder cannot read your password. Again, if you make an error before pressing the *return* or *enter* key you can use the *backspace* and *delete* keys to correct your error. Otherwise, if you mis-type either the user name or the password, most log-in programs will allow you to have another go. Once you have entered a user name and the correct corresponding password, you are said to have 'logged-in'. You are then ready to use the LAN facilities.

If you need to change your password for any reason, this is a good time to do so. On a Macintosh, you will often be given the opportunity to change the password after logging-in, within the Chooser option (Figure 2.2). You may also be given the opportunity to store your user name and password on the Macintosh, so that it automatically logs you in to the LAN when you power up your computer.

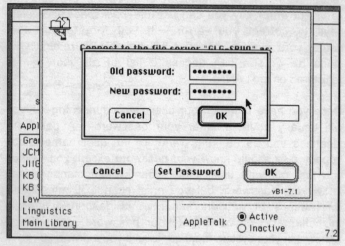

Figure 2.2 Changing your password on a Macintosh.

On a PC you may be able to change the password from within *Windows* or you may have to go to the DOS prompt and type a command like 'password', 'passwd', 'pass', or 'set password'. If in doubt, consult your LAN system manager.

When you change your password, you must normally type in the old one first, so that it is impossible for someone to wander up to your logged-in computer whilst you are out of the room and change your password. You must then type in the new password twice (Figure 2.3). If the two passwords are not identical, the password program recognises that they cannot both be correct, and that you must have mis-typed one or both of them. The password program will not accept the changes, and you will have to start again.

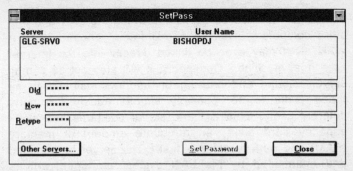

*Figure 2.3 Changing your password on a PC using
Novell NetWare.*

The Server

As described in Chapter 1, some LANs rely on a dedicated
server computer (server-based LANs), whilst others
manage without (peer-to-peer LANs). A server computer
serves the LAN by providing it with a whole range of
services, and these are described in this section.
However, since there is no dedicated server computer in
a peer-to-peer LAN, the various functions normally
provided by a server are shared out between all the
computers that comprise the LAN.

The server computer controls who logs-in, i.e. it checks
user names and passwords against the lists it has stored
on its hard disks. So when you log-in to the LAN, what
you are doing is logging-in to the server computer. The
server controls which LAN devices may be used, which
files may be accessed, edited and executed. The server
houses and runs the core network operating system
software, and has all the shared network software and
other shared software located on its hard disks. Usually,
all the main network hardware devices are physically
connected to the server, such as printers, plotters, CD-
ROMs, scanners, etc.

The server will also be the link between the LAN and any other computers, such as a mainframe, another LAN, a WAN, or it may even be linked directly into the Internet as a host machine. Commonly, it will also act as a mail server, storing and passing on users' e-mail. With all these tasks to do, possibly simultaneously for many different users, it helps if the server computer has high-capacity hard disks, an adequate amount of memory (RAM) and runs reasonably fast. The server is managed and maintained by the LAN system manager, who is responsible for keeping it running efficiently, night and day.

Disk Drives

If you have a PC, and you are not connected to a LAN, then you will normally have access to a maximum of three disk drives, and a minimum of two disk drives. You will have a hard disk drive built into your machine, which is normally called the C: drive. You may also have a 5.25" floppy disk drive and/or a 3.5" floppy disk drive, at the front of your machine (Figure 2.4). These are normally called the A: and B: drives. On a Macintosh, your hard disk drive is accessed via an icon labelled 'Hard Disk', by default, although this may be changed to anything you want, simply by over-typing the label panel. Normally only 3.5" floppy disks may be inserted at the front of a Macintosh, and these appear as a named disk icon on screen. The hard disk and floppy disk drives are essentially for your personal use.

The hard disk in your computer is where the computer's operating system is stored. In the case of a PC, this is DOS, and possibly a higher-level operating system like *Windows* or *OS/2*. In the case of a Macintosh, this is *System 7* . The hard disk may also be used for storage of your personal files and applications. In a server-based LAN these personal files and applications are normally only accessible from your computer, although your system manager may have some access via the LAN.

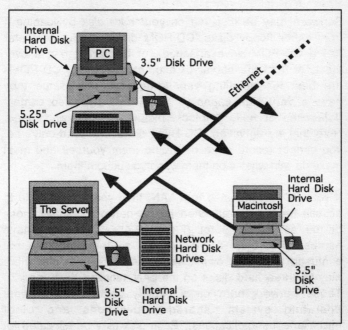

Figure 2.4 Disk drives in a server-based LAN.

If you are running your computer as part of a LAN, there will also be some LAN communications software installed on your hard disk, and probably some LAN applications. These are normally installed by your system manager, along with any other software packages provided by your institution.

Floppy disks (diskettes) may be used for keeping back-ups of personal software and data files, since hard disks can sometimes fail. However, you should not need to keep back-ups of network software and other software that is provided by your institution. If you should accidentally lose these, your system manager should be able re-install them.

Software may be installed on your hard disk by loading it from either floppy disks, CD-ROM disks (if your computer has a CD-ROM drive attached), or by transferring it over the LAN from the server or another computer. CD-ROMs are best for installing very large programs, since they have a very high capacity. CD-ROMs can also contain databases of text, graphics, pictures, sound and video. Note that by definition, CD-ROM disks are 'read-only', i.e. you cannot record extra data onto them yourself and must make do with what is on them when you bought them.

If your PC is connected to a LAN, then you may be able to access hard disks attached to the network, usually those of the server computer (Figure 2.4). These will have names other than A:, B:, or C:, so that they are not confused with your own disk drives. For example, there may be three hard disks on the LAN, labelled X:, Y: and Z:. These network hard disks usually contain the network operating system, shared applications and other miscellaneous applications. Each disk may be allocated for different purposes, e.g. the X: drive may contain the network operating system software, the Y: drive may contain users' personal files, and the Z: drive may contain certain software packages. To access these disks in *Windows*, run the File Manager application, and they should be shown alongside your computer's disk drives as extra network drives (Figure 2.5).

In DOS, you may only need to type the name of the network disk drive in order to access it. Macintosh users must select the network disk drives and other LAN devices using the Chooser. They could have any name, so, if in doubt, ask your LAN system manager.

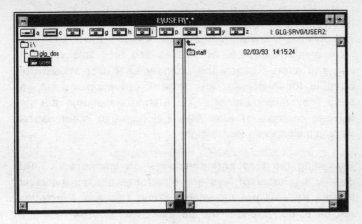

*Figure 2.5 Choosing network disk drives in
Windows.*

The network hard disks also contain personal directories
belonging to each LAN user, known as 'home directories'.
Users may keep their files in their home directories as
well as on the hard disk of their own computer. The home
directory, user name and password are collectively
referred to as an 'account'. This is broadly similar to a
bank account, which also has a 'home directory' (the
account itself), a user name (the account name, or
account number) and a password (a signature, or cash
card PIN number).

Note that in some simpler networks you will not
necessarily be able to access shared network hard disk
drives, although you will be able to use other network
resources, such as printers. In a very simple network
set-up, you may only be able use your Macintosh or PC to
log-in to another, multi-user computer, such as a Unix
workstation or a mainframe computer, so that you can
use the resources on that machine.

Network Privileges

The system manager controls the access privileges you have on the LAN, i.e. which files and programs you can use and alter. Clearly the ordinary LAN user should not be able to tinker with the network operating system, in case they might damage it. Also, they should not be allowed to read or alter files belonging to other users, without their specific permission.

Try listing the files and directories on the network hard disks. A number of files and directories are not available to you, and will not be listed. Some files and directories will be listed, but you will be denied all access to them. Other files, you may be able to read or execute, but not edit or change in any way. However, you should be able to do anything to the files and directories that reside in your home directory, as you can with files and directories on your computer's hard disk, since these 'belong' to you. In fact, the only two people who can access and change files in any home directory will normally be the system manager and the legitimate user of that home directory.

If it is important for you to have access to some particular files or directories on the LAN, you should see your system manager, who may give you such privileges. Alternatively, the system manager may make a copy of the files or directories and put them in your home directory, so that you can have full access to them.

File Sharing

In a server-based LAN, the hard disk drive on your computer (i.e. disk drive C:, or the 'Hard Disk') is generally only accessible to you. There are exceptions, however. Some server-based network operating systems provide the system manager with access to the hard disk drives of all networked computers (Figure 2.6). This is so that the system manager can more easily maintain the software on each networked computer, and may check on the applications people are running, to ensure that they do not conflict with the smooth running of the LAN.

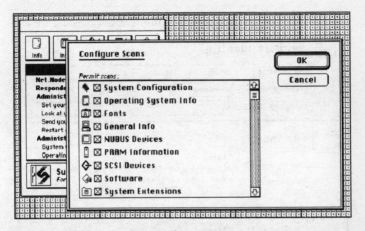

Figure 2.6 Controlling system manager access to a Macintosh.

Some server-based network operating systems also allow you to permit other users to share files on your hard disk drive. For example, on a Macintosh, you would switch on the 'File Sharing' option under 'Control Panels' (Figure 2.7). Your Macintosh should be given a name and a password, so that when other Macintosh users log-in to the LAN, they will have the option to select your Macintosh, and 'log-in' provided they know the password. They then have access to your files.

Peer-to-peer LANs usually have a well-developed system for sharing hard disks, directories and files. In principle, any LAN user can access any file on any hard disk of any computer in the LAN. In practice, other users will restrict access rights to their hard disks, directories and files. For example, a file or directory may be set as read-only, or may be read-only for certain named LAN users. Alternatively, a file may be set so that it is not accessible to any other computer, so that it is effectively a 'hidden' file.

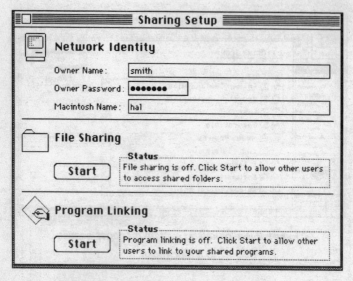

Figure 2.7 File sharing control on a Macintosh.

Printers

Most server-based LANs have a printer physically attached to the server computer. In a peer-to-peer LAN, there will normally be a printer attached to one of the computers that is designated as the main network printer for all users. The network printer must be capable of producing a large amount of output quickly, since it must cope with the demands of several users. Commonly the network printer is a fast laser printer. Sometimes LAN users will have the luxury of several different printers to choose from. Your PC or Macintosh will send all documents to be printed to whichever has been set as the default printer. If there is more than one network printer, it should be possible to select which printer you wish to use, by selecting the name of the printer (Figure 2.8). Networked printers are always named. Most laser printers have more than one feeder tray, so that output can be produced on different media such as paper and overhead transparencies, and also on different sizes and orientations of paper (or transparencies). In this case, the different trays are usually given different names on the LAN, as if they were different printers.

On a Macintosh, the name of the printer you wish to use may be selected using the 'Chooser' menu.

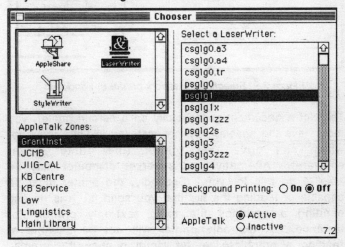

Figure 2.8 Selecting a network printer with the Apple Chooser.

In *Windows* printers can be normally be selected using the 'Print Manager' application (Figure 2.9), although this depends on how your LAN has been configured. If no network printers are listed by the Print Manager, ask your system manager for help.

The Chooser and the Print Manager provide an easy way of finding out what printers are available on your LAN, as well as a way of selecting them. In DOS there are several possible ways of accessing the network printer, and you should consult your system manager about the best way.

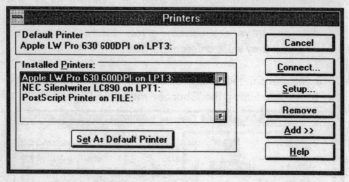

Figure 2.9 Selecting a network printer in Windows.

To print a document successfully on a certain printer, you must have the special software installed in your computer which can drive that printer (the printer driver software). Alternatively, the server computer may be able to do this for you. Secondly, the printer must be capable of reading the file that you send it. It is no use sending a graphics file to a text-only printer, for instance. A text-only printer will not be capable of reading a graphics file, let alone printing it correctly. Text and graphics files can be coded for printing in a variety of ways, and these are sometimes called 'printer languages' or 'printer formats'. Some printers are able to handle a variety of languages, but you must check to see whether the printer of interest to you can handle the output from your program. Probably the most common printer language in everyday use on PC and Macintosh LANs is *PostScript*. Most good software can produce *PostScript* output, and most laser-printers can handle *PostScript*.

When you send a document to be printed on a server-based LAN, it is common for it to be copied to a hard disk drive attached to the server. This copying procedure is called 'spooling'. The document can then be passed to the printer when the printer is ready, and you can carry on using your computer whilst you wait for the document to be printed. This is all handled by special 'print spooler' software.

In a peer-to-peer LAN, the document to be printed can, in theory, be sent to any of the printers attached to any of the networked computers. In practice, some users may have made their printers off-limits to other users. Clearly, the person whose computer is handling the printing may be inconvenienced by their computer slowing-down whilst printing is taking place, and it will also interfere with them carrying out their own printing.

As documents are sent to the server for printing, they are usually given a print 'job number' for reference, and they are placed in a printer queue. The order that these documents or jobs are printed depends on a system of priority which is set up by the system manager. Print jobs from certain users or certain file types may have higher priority. Usually, large print jobs have a very low priority, since it is generally preferable to get small print jobs done quickly, and leave the larger jobs until the network is less busy.

All LAN users will be able to examine the print queue, provided they have the right network software installed (Figure 2.10, 2.11). If problems arise with printing certain documents, the system manager and/or the sender of the document should be informed, so that the offending document can be removed from the printer queue, or given a different priority.

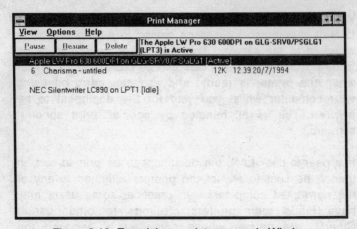

Figure 2.10 Examining a printer queue in Windows.

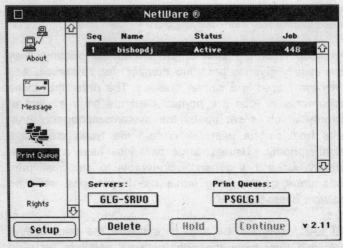

*Figure 2.11 Examining a printer queue on a
Macintosh using Novell NetWare.*

The cost of printing documents, i.e. paper, toner, etc.,
must be met by someone. Ask your system manager how
much it costs to use each of the available network
printers. Colour printers are usually the most expensive

to use. It is often worth doing a test printout of your document on a monochrome printer before sending your document to the colour printer. As well as controlling the printers, the server computer may also do the accounting by keeping a tally of how much printing is done by each user, and on which printers. From this information, the system manager can calculate the cost of each user's printing, at regular intervals. How printing costs are covered will depend on the policy of the organisation. On some LANs it can be quite complicated to keep track of each user's expenditure, and some system managers resort to keeping 'honesty' books next to each printer, where users can write down how many copies they have produced, each time they use the printer.

Copying and Moving Files

Copying and moving files between your hard disk and the network disk drives can be as simple as copying and moving files between directories on your hard disk, or between your hard disk drive and your floppy disk drive. On a Macintosh, you need only open up the network hard disk icon, open your hard disk icon, open the folders of interest, and then drag and drop the file. Several may be selected at once and moved together. In *Windows*, files can be copied or moved between hard disks using the File Manager, either by dragging and dropping them into folders, or by re-naming them. In DOS, the normal commands for copying and moving files should work, but remember to include the intended disk drive name in the new file path name, be it C:, X:, Y: or whatever. Remember that your use of files on the LAN depends on privileges and file ownership, so that you may not be able to copy some files, or if you can, you might not be able to use them. Note also that copying software off the LAN may infringe the software licence agreement. Check with your LAN system manager before helping yourself to software that you find on the LAN. On some LANs it may be necessary to use a special network program to move and copy files, such a File Transfer Protocol (FTP) program. FTP is explained in Chapter 4.

Other Network Users

There are LAN applications for PCs and Macintoshes that allow you to interrogate the server and find out the user names of other users presently logged-in to the LAN. For example, there is a Novell *NetWare* utility that allows you to do this in *Windows* (Figure 2.12). Furthermore, you can type in a short message (1-2 lines or so), which will then be delivered immediately to any named user (Figure 2.13).

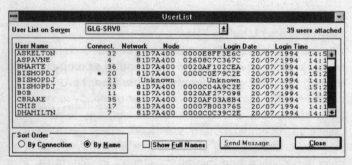

Figure 2.12 Using Novell NetWare and Windows to produce a list of current LAN users.

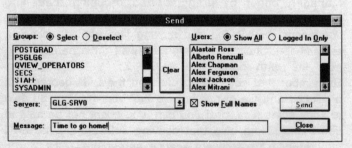

Figure 2.13 Sending a message across the LAN, using Novell NetWare and Windows.

The message will appear on their screen, on top of any work that they might be doing. Once they have read the message, they can dismiss it with a keystroke, and the message is destroyed. On some LANs it is possible to send a 'broadcast' message of this kind to all users currently logged-in to the LAN.

Longer messages should be sent to other users via an electronic mail (e-mail) program, such as *Eudora*, Microsoft *Mail* or *Pegasus Mail*. E-mail is described fully in Chapter 5. However, there is one main difference when using e-mail on a LAN, which is that a full e-mail address is not normally necessary. A user name only will suffice as the delivery address.

Some packages, such as Microsoft *Mail*, are particularly well designed for sending messages within a LAN. Microsoft *Mail* allows you to send 'notes' to other LAN users, with any kind of file attached. Such files are called 'attachments' or 'enclosures' (Figure 2.14).

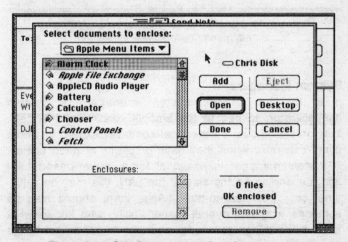

Figure 2.14 Sending a note and enclosure across a LAN, using Microsoft Mail on a Macintosh.

Microsoft *Mail* also allows you to leave telephone messages and place travel booking requests, which may be a useful facility within a larger company or organisation that has a travel office connected to the LAN, or a secretary responsible for making travel arrangements (Figure 2.15).

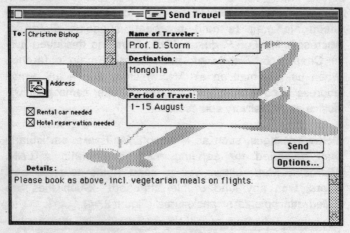

Figure 2.15 Making a travel booking on a LAN, using Microsoft Mail on a Macintosh.

System Managers

It is the job of the system manager, or system administrator, to see to the smooth running of the LAN. This person should be the local computer expert, to whom users can refer when they have problems or need advice. A system manager is essential for a server-based LAN and, depending on the size of the LAN, this may be a full-time job. For peer-to-peer LANs, there should also be someone who has overall responsibility, who knows what to do when things go wrong, and who to call to get things fixed.

The system manager of a server-based LAN has a number of responsibilities, which include hardware and software maintenance, user accounts, running the server, making back-ups, and maintaining security. The system manager has the maximum privilege possible, which means he or she can examine, edit, move and delete any file on the server, and in some LANs, any file on any computer hard disk on the LAN. Sometimes the system manager is said to have 'root access', or to be the 'root user'. Clearly it is a responsible and powerful position along the lines of a 'Big Brother', which should never be abused.

The system manager makes sure that all the computers and peripheral devices are correctly connected and interacting properly with the LAN. Most of the critical software will be lodged on the hard disk drives of the server machine, and the peripheral devices will generally be connected to the server. Hence, it is especially important that the server is correctly configured and running smoothly, for the whole LAN depends on it. The server should be running 24 hours a day, so that people can always use the LAN, even if they choose to work late at night.

In addition, each computer on the LAN must be given a unique identity number and name, so that it can be recognised by the server and other networked machines. It is easier for both users and the system manager to remember a name, rather than a number, but each computer should have both. More detail is given about computer names and numbers in Chapter 4.

Every person who uses the LAN should be registered with the system manager, who will provide them with a user name, password and an account. The user may change their password themselves, but not their user name. Normally, there should be no need to change a user name, but the system manager can do this if it is really necessary. When you cease to be a user on the LAN, you should inform the system manager, and he or she will remove your details from the server.

The system manager is responsible for the software on the LAN, making sure that it is properly installed, and that licence agreements are upheld. The system manager will install new versions of the software as they become available, and make sure that there are no conflicting software packages installed on the system, which might cause problems. Users of the system need to be kept informed of developments on the LAN, and to this end many system managers establish a message system that gives the user the latest information when the user logs-in to the LAN. This is often called 'the message of the day'.

The system manager should also issue messages over the network, should any major problems arise, for example, if they have to shut the server machine down for maintenance. Users should get ample warning of a server shutdown, so that they may stop using programs, data, and devices over the network, and log-out of the LAN. Normally, the system manager will set up a program on the server so that warnings of the impending shutdown are sent to all users currently logged-in to the LAN, at regular intervals before shutdown actually occurs (e.g. at 10, 5, 2 and 1 minutes prior to shutdown).

The system manager will create back-ups of the server's hard disk drives on a regular basis, usually daily or weekly, so that if the hard disk drives should fail, the amount of data lost will be limited. The back-ups can be used to re-install data and other files onto the hard disk drives when they are either fixed or replaced. Back-ups will usually be made by copying the information stored on the hard disks onto other hard disks, a tape drive machine or diskettes. Tape drives are favoured, because they have a very high capacity, typically 2-5 GB.

It is not the system manager's responsibility to make back-ups of the disk drive on your own personal machine. They may show you how to do it once, but after that it is your own responsibility. Most people find that copying their personal files and applications onto a number of diskettes is the most convenient way to make a back-up. Note that you do not need to make back-up copies of network operating software, network applications and other applications that have been provided for you by your LAN system manager, since he or she will be able to re-install these should they get lost or corrupted. You should make back-ups on a regular basis, at least every couple of weeks. Hard disks are quite reliable these days, but are not infallible, and do crash from time to time. Also, human error (i.e. your error) may mean that precious data files become lost or overwritten, in which case you will be very glad that you have a back-up.

Network Security

The system manager will give you a user name, and probably a password, when you join your computer to a LAN. You should change your password immediately, or enter one if there is not one already allocated as explained earlier in this chapter. It is important that you, and you alone, know your password. Never let other people use your user name and password. Even if you trust them, there is no telling who else they might give your password to, or they might carelessly write it down somewhere conspicuous. Also, be wary of leaving your computer whilst it is logged-in, to go for a tea-break or whatever. It only takes a few minutes for someone else to sit down at your computer and create havoc.

Any damage that is caused by someone using your user name and password, whether you gave them permission or not, will be attributed to you, whether you like it or not. Any messages sent across the LAN, e-mail and contributions to Network News groups will all be attributed to you and you will have to bear the responsibility for any libel suits! Also, it is not fair on the other users of the LAN, to have an unauthorised person using the LAN, and possibly causing problems. Your system manager will be justifiably displeased, if you are found to be flaunting this very basic rule!

Therefore, guard your password carefully. You should also change it regularly, at least every few months, just in case other people have discovered what it is. Some systems will force you to change your password at regular intervals, perhaps every six months or year. If you forget your password, the system manager will be able to provide you with a new one. They will not be able to tell you the old one, since when your password is entered onto the system, a special program on the server encrypts it before storing it in a password file.

The encryption method is not reversible, so it is not possible to create the original password from the encrypted version. When you log-in to the LAN, the password you enter is encrypted, and then compared with the encrypted version which is lodged against your user name in the password file. If they match, then you are allowed into the LAN.

There have been cases of people breaking the encryption method in order to gain unauthorised access to computer networks. This is done by copying the file of encrypted network passwords. A computer is then used to create encrypted versions of all the words in a dictionary, using the same encryption method. The encrypted passwords can be compared with those produced from the dictionary, and the original passwords deduced. For this reason, it is important that your password is not a word normally found in a dictionary. This can best be done by using a mixture of alphabetic and numeric characters. Many systems will even let you use punctuation characters in your password. Also, make sure your password is not too short, because this would make it easier for someone determined to discover it. Many LANs will now not allow you to use a password with less than a minimum number of characters, or a password that does not include at least some non-alphabetic characters.

Virus Protection

Computer viruses are small programs that are so called because they behave in a similar way to the viruses caught by humans and other animals. They are capable of self-replication and are good at disguising themselves. Worst of all, they can be very destructive. Viruses are written by anarchic programmers around the world, who seem to get some sense of satisfaction from spreading misery amongst the rest of us. Although virus creation borders on being a criminal activity, it is practically impossible to locate the perpetrators. Furthermore, since viruses replicate themselves, they can, in theory, survive almost indefinitely in a large population of computers. Some common viruses have been around for many years.

Most computer viruses spread via the interchange of floppy disks between computers. Some viruses can only exist on floppy disks, whilst others can copy themselves onto your hard disks. Some viruses can inadvertently be transferred onto your computer when transferring other files across the network. Viruses commonly disguise themselves by 'hiding' in certain sectors of a floppy disk, or by attaching themselves to another program file, which in itself may be harmless. Thus, if a program file is found to be larger than it should be, this may indicate that a virus has attached itself.

Viruses manifest themselves in a variety of ways too numerous to describe, since there are now thousands of them. Fortunately, few of them are very common. They sometimes remain dormant until some particular operation is carried out on your computer, or they may wait for a certain date to arrive before activating (they can do this by querying the on-board computer clock). When they are activated they may do something relatively harmless, such as print a rude message on the screen. More commonly they will scramble other files on a disk, or cause problems when saving files.

Luckily, there are now a whole host of programs available that can detect and destroy viruses. These programs are available from computer archives around the world and from network system managers. Most of them are freeware or shareware. There are also some commercial anti-virus programs for sale. Well-known examples are *Sam Intercept* and *F-Prot*. Once installed, you can run these programs at any time, and instruct them to scan your hard disk, floppy disks, and computer memory for viruses. Most anti-virus programs can also be set up so that they check your hard disks and memory on start-up of your computer, they check any floppy disks that are inserted, and will regularly check memory. They are capable of recognising a very wide variety of viruses, and at your command will generally be able to destroy them and repair your disks and files. Some programs will also spot new viruses and pieces of suspicious code that just might be a new virus. In this case, they will warn you, even though they may be unable to do anything about it.

The importance of having an anti-virus program installed on your computer cannot be over-stressed. More than that, you should make sure that it is properly installed and used regularly. Be particularly sure to keep all your floppy disks free of viruses, and check any new ones that you get. Even brand new floppy disks have been known to contain viruses, although this is rare, and if you use only reputable brands you should be safe. Viruses are much more common on PCs than Macintoshes, but users of both should take care. Not only are you protecting yourself and your own system, but you are also stopping the spread of viruses. This is particularly important in a networked environment. If you are in doubt about any particular software or floppy disks, or the health of your computer (e.g. it might be behaving strangely for no particular reason), then inform your network system manager immediately. They will be able to help you check to see if a virus is present, and will help you eradicate it. It is very much in their interests also to keep the network free of viruses.

Chapter 3

NETWORK HARDWARE AND SOFTWARE

In an ideal world, a LAN user should only need to know how to use a LAN, but not how the LAN is constructed and how it works. However, since many LANs are far from perfect, it is often useful to have a basic understanding of what comprises a LAN, even if it is only to enable you to conduct a meaningful conversation with your LAN system manager! In this chapter the most commonly used LAN hardware and software is described, for both Macintoshes and PCs. The distinction between hardware and software is the most important to grasp, but also dealt with are the various types of software used on a network. The most popular communication protocols and network operating systems are described.

PC Network Hardware

There are several ways to connect a PC LAN, although connections using Ethernet technology (described below) are, by far, the most common. An alternative to Ethernet is the Token Ring system from IBM, which can be slightly faster, but is more expensive. Networks can also be created by connecting PCs via their serial ports, their parallel ports, or by using Arcnet, all of which are very much slower than either Ethernet or Token Ring. Arcnet is an old networking standard, which uses coaxial cables and a special expansion card for each machine. Most networking software for PCs is designed to use Ethernet.

Ethernet was developed by the Xerox Corporation, and was named after the theoretical luminiferous ether through which electromagnetic radiation was once thought to propagate. It was first used to connect the Xerox Alto computers in 1973. Ethernet technology has been standardised by Xerox, Digital Equipment and Intel, who drew up an agreement known as IEEE (Institution of Electrical and Electronic Engineers) standard 802.3.

Ethernet comprises specialised cables, electronic adapter cards, and software to run the LAN. Adapter cards are generally fitted internally by pushing them into a specially designed expansion slot inside the computer. The Ethernet cable can then be connected to the rear of the computer using a special connection, often a 'T'-shaped device. Portable and laptop computers are often too small to have an internal adapter card, so it may be necessary to have an external adapter card housed in a separate box, which is connected between the computer and the Ethernet cable.

There is a large variety of Ethernet adapter cards available, but good networking software such Microsoft *Windows NT* and *Windows for Workgroups* can usually drive any of the leading brand adapter cards. Some cards have to be manually adjusted for optimum performance, by changing jumpers or switches on the card itself. It is preferable to use cards that can be controlled entirely by the software running on the computer. 8-bit and 16-bit adapter cards are both available, but the 16-bit adapters are worth the extra cost, since they provide an increase in speed and LAN performance. 32-bit adapter cards are only worthwhile for a server machine on a large LAN. Currently the industry standard for PC Ethernet cards is Novell or Eagle NE2000.

There are three types of Ethernet cable, all of which require different adapter cards. These are Thick, Thin and Twisted-Pair cables. Thick Ethernet cable (also known as Standard Ethernet and 10base5) is commonly used since its coaxial design provides good signal quality. It is bright yellow or orange in colour, approximately 1/2 inch in diameter and is specifically designed for Ethernet transmissions. Thin Ethernet (also known as Cheapernet and 10base2), is even more commonly used, because of its easy installation and reduced cabling cost. Thin Ethernet has a diameter of approximately 1/4 inch. Twisted-Pair Ethernet (also known as 10base-T) is the newest of the three standards, finalised in 1990. Twisted-Pair Ethernet cables are similar to standard telephone wiring, and are easier to install. However, each networked computer must be directly connected to a central 'hub', a piece of hardware that is quite expensive. Twisted-Pair Ethernet cables are also available with shielding that prevents electronic eavesdropping. This latter feature is very useful when data security is important, such as in a commercial or military environment.

Macintosh Network Hardware
LANs that comprise only Macintosh computers may use Apple's own *LocalTalk* network system. The *LocalTalk* system is only suitable for Macintoshes and Apple peripherals, whereas Ethernet can connect mixed LANs, which might include other sorts of computers, such as PCs.

The attraction of a *LocalTalk* LAN is its comparative cheapness and ease of installation. Every Macintosh has a built-in *LocalTalk* transceiver, making the task of creating a network quite simple. However, *LocalTalk* limits the speed of LAN traffic to 230.4 Kb/s, whereas Ethernet can transmit data at up to 10 Mb/s. Consequently, Ethernet is potentially about forty times faster. However, the actual difference in speed depends on the amount of activity on the LAN, and the kind of software controlling the LAN. In practice, Ethernet is often only two to five times faster than *LocalTalk*. In addition, an Ethernet has a higher bandwidth, i.e. it can cope with more computers on the LAN, sending information around the LAN at the same time. With *LocalTalk* you will start noticing an appreciable loss of performance if more than 10 Macintoshes are using the LAN. Thus, *LocalTalk* is best suited to small LANs, in which speed is not the prime consideration. Apple also support Ethernet technology with their *EtherTalk* application (Figure 3.1).

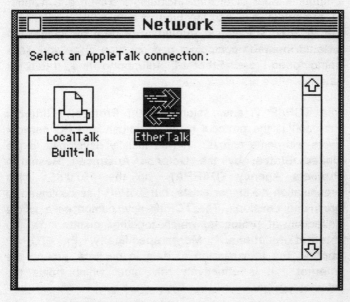

Figure 3.1 Choosing EtherTalk or LocalTalk using a network control panel on a Macintosh.

Apple also supports the Token Ring LAN system popularised by IBM. Apple produces a special Token Ring adapter card and software to run it.

Communication Protocols

PCs, Macintoshes and other types of computers communicate using a few standard communication protocols. Communication protocols are essentially primitive computer languages that allow computers to exchange data, even if they are different types of computer. Without communication protocols, networks would not be possible. The standards have been agreed by the major hardware manufacturers, software developers, standards organisations and other interested parties. The most suitable protocol for any given situation depends on a large number of factors, including the type and number of computers involved, the type of data being exchanged, the required speed and frequency of data exchange, the distance between computers and the type of network links being used, e.g. Ethernet, telephone line, radio or satellite.

The TCP/IP (Transmission Control Protocol / Internet Protocol) is the protocol most Macintosh and PC network users will come across. It was initially developed in the United States, by the Defense Advanced Research Projects Agency (DARPA) in the 1970's. This organisation no longer exists, but TCP/IP has continued to grow and develop. The TCP/IP now comprises a whole collection of protocols, which together dictate how the Internet functions. More specifically, the TCP/IP controls the transmission of data in packets, around the Internet. It is effectively the 'glue' which holds the Internet together.

Much currently available network software is dependent on a TCP/IP program being installed on your Macintosh or PC. A commonly used TCP/IP program for PCs is *Trumpet*. Apple's implementation of this protocol is *MacTCP*, which serves a similar purpose. The latter has been around for a while, but now comes as standard with Apple's *System 7.5* (Figure 3.2).

TCP/IP can also be used by people with modems. For this, they will need to install another program that uses either SL/IP (Serial Line / Internet Protocol) or the slightly better PPP (Point-to-Point Protocol). A PPP program for PCs is NCSA *PPP*. Macintosh programs include the commercial *MacSLIP*, and the freeware programs *InterSLIP* and *MacPPP*. These programs allow PC or Macintosh computers to become full Internet hosts when they are connected via a modem to the Internet.

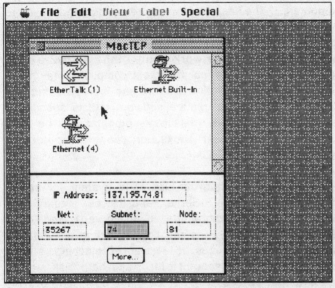

Figure 3.2 A MacTCP network control panel.

There are other communication protocols compatible with TCP/IP, which are used for specific tasks. These include Telnet, FTP (File Transfer Protocol), and SMTP (Simple Mail Transfer Protocol), and permit remote access and control of computers, transfer of data and files, and transfer of electronic mail respectively. These protocols can be implemented in software for PCs, Macintoshes and other computers too, in order to promote easy communications.

Network Operating Systems

In addition to communication protocols, there are network operating systems, which are much higher-level languages that allow system managers to control a LAN, and LAN users to have access to network facilities and communications. Many software manufacturers produce network operating systems for server-based LAN client computers. The major manufacturers also produce more powerful software for server computers, intended for use with their own brand of client software. However, rival brands of network operating software are sometimes compatible, so that client computers may run a different brand of software from the server computer. Some manufacturers produce software that is specifically for peer-to-peer LANs, while other products can be used on either peer-to-peer LANs, or client computers of server-based LANs.

Microsoft's current network operating system for server computers is called *NT Server*, and this can interact with both PCs and Macintoshes in a server-based LAN. Microsoft *Windows NT* is the corresponding software for client PCs, and requires at least a 486 machine, a large amount of memory (about 16 MB), and hard disk storage space (about 75-100 MB). Since many users do not have such high specification PCs, a more commonly used product is Microsoft *Windows for Workgroups*.

Microsoft's *Windows for Workgroups* is a specially written version of Microsoft *Windows*, that can be used by PCs in a peer-to-peer LAN, or a server-based LAN. *Windows for Workgroups* often comes bundled with new PCs, in the same way that previous versions of *Windows* used to be, making this a popular choice of networking software. When installed on a stand-alone PC, the software automatically detects that there is no network attached, and network facilities remain inactive. When the PC is attached to a network, the software will automatically detect the adapter card and install the relevant software to run it. *Windows for Workgroups* will use Ethernet and Token Ring adapters. It can also happily coexist with Novell's networking software. Available facilities include electronic mail, a group office calendar, and the ability to share a single printer amongst the entire LAN. An add-on feature is the ability to share access to a fax modem, which is useful, but does cost extra, and is rather slow. Many people prefer to use existing *Windows* fax programs such as *Winfax*. *Windows for Workgroups* allows other users access to your directories if you wish, but access is on an 'all or nothing' basis and you cannot then make specific files and subdirectories within those directories off-limits. There is a 'chat' facility that allows LAN users to communicate by sending text interactively to each other. Included with the package is a copy of Microsoft *Mail*, which is also available separately, and is a powerful e-mail application in its own right. One of the drawbacks of *Windows for Workgroups* is its lack of security in the default installation, but in a small business this is unlikely to cause problems.

A recent development is *Windows 95* which is a comprehensive new version of *Windows* with full networking facilities. The minimum specification you should need to run *Windows 95* is a 486 based PC with 4-8 MB of RAM and as large a hard disk as you can afford, fortunately these are becoming increasingly less expensive.

IBM have recently produced a new version of their *OS/2* operating system, called *OS/2 Warp*, which has advanced networking capabilities as well as more typical LAN facilities. A particular feature of this system is easy and rapid access to the Internet.

Novell also produces a network operating system for installation on a PC server, called *NetWare,* and an equivalent for a Macintosh server, called *NetWare for*

Macintosh. *NetWare* can be used to operate a LAN comprising PCs running Microsoft *Windows*, DOS and IBM *OS/2*, as well as Macintosh machines and a variety of Unix-based workstations. *NetWare* can handle TCP/IP and *AppleTalk* protocols.

In addition to routine LAN management tasks, *NetWare* has some other noteworthy features. The latest version has a file compression facility that can automatically compress files on the server machine's hard disks until they are needed, when they can then be uncompressed. This can more than double the effective space available on the hard disks. Another feature of this software is password security, which is very high, since a special method is employed whereby passwords are never passed over the LAN cables, thus preventing electronic eavesdropping. Also, the system can be set up to provide some users, called 'auditors', with special privileges and some of the powers of a system manager. Users can access a *Netware* LAN using a variety of languages, including English, French, Italian, German and Spanish. Network printers may be attached to any client machine, as well as the server machine. The operating system also supports CD-ROMs and read/write optical storage disk units on the LAN. There is a well-developed messaging system for *NetWare* users, together with a basic e-mail package called *First Mail*. At the time of writing, the latest version of *NetWare* was *Netware 4*.

Also available is *NetWare SFT III*, which is a specialised version of *NetWare*. It is extremely reliable and particularly suitable for commercial applications where the LAN should never be inoperative due to a fault. This software insures against the LAN becoming unavailable, by actually using two servers on the LAN, one of which can always act as a back-up, if the first should fail. The user is normally unaware of this as the two servers 'appear' as one on the LAN.

The complementary Novell network client software is called *Personal NetWare*, which can be used within peer-to-peer LANs (of up to 50 machines) or on client machines in a server-based LAN. Versions exist for users of DOS, *Windows* and Macintosh machines. Each user has an account on the LAN, regardless of the number of machines, which is not always the case for peer-to-peer LANs. Log-ins can be restricted to certain machines for security purposes. Logging-in to an account provides access to all LAN resources, such as files, printers and other devices, although access may be restricted for certain users. Access to each LAN directory for any given user can be defined to be either 'full' (i.e. 'read and write'), 'read-only', 'write-only' or 'none'. The accessibility can be set by the owner of the directory. The right to use each shared printer may be set to be either 'full' or 'none' for each user. The LAN manager can make changes to the LAN configuration and the privileges of LAN users through a special 'supervisor' account. Each user account is replicated on all the networked machines, so that if one is turned off, the rest can continue functioning without interruption. When such a machine is switched back on again, all users are automatically reconnected with it.

Personal NetWare offers basic communication facilities, with a rudimentary messaging system that allows short messages to be sent to other users, but with no automatic reply facility. Resources on the LAN such as hard disks, printers and CD-ROMs, can be controlled quite easily. Network information and diagnostics can be supplied at any networked machine, including a graphic map of the LAN. LAN administration is one of *Personal Netware*'s strongest features. A system manager can control the LAN from any one of the networked computers. Within a server-based LAN, *Personal NetWare* works best when the server is running Novell *NetWare*. However, it can also be used in a LAN that has a rival operating system installed on the server, such as Microsoft *NT Server*.

Artisoft have two products, called *LANtastic* and *Simply LANtastic*. The latter can be installed on PCs in a peer-to-peer LAN, and is compatible with DOS and *Windows*. However, it is worth noting that you must use Artisoft's own network cable and adapter cards. The *Simply LANtastic* system is fairly basic, but is easy to use. Under *Simply LANtastic* there is no concept of individual users, only of the actual computers networked together. The only way of exchanging information between computers is by using the rudimentary mailbox service. The software is an ideal introduction for network novices.

For more advanced features, *Simply LANtastic* can be upgraded to the full system, which is called *LANtastic*. This software is designed to work in either a peer-to-peer LAN, or on client machines in a server-based LAN, and can work in conjunction with server software such as that described above. You are also able to use Ethernet adapter cards other than those sold by Artisoft. Compared to *Windows for Workgroups*, this package can offer more in terms of network security and e-mail, and can be used by *Windows*, DOS and Macintosh users (*LANtastic for Macintosh*). Also included in *LANtastic* is a diary and schedule making facility for individuals and a group of users.

Other network operating systems include *ENS for NetWare,* and the more advanced *Vines* system, which are both made by Banyan, and IBM's *LAN Server* that is based on their *OS/2* windows-based operating system. These latter network operating systems are primarily for PC LANs.

Network Application Software

There is a vast and increasing range of free and commercial software that makes use of computer LANs. This software is generally available for both Macintoshes and PCs, and provides various extra facilities for LAN users, such as file transfer, electronic mail, and network games. These programs are often called 'network applications' and should not be confused with either communication protocols or network operating systems. Network applications rely on your computer being physically connected to a computer LAN, with the appropriate communications software already installed and running. Without this they cannot function.

Once your computer is connected to a LAN with the appropriate hardware and software, you can then install as many network applications as you like on your computer, provided your machine has enough memory and hard disk space. Some of these programs are described or mentioned in the following chapters of this book, although there are many thousands more. Installing network applications is not always straightforward, since you may have to set up the software so that it knows the names and numbers of other machines on the LAN, and other technical parameters. Also, you must be sure that the network applications you install can utilise the communications protocols and network operating system that you are running, otherwise they may not function properly, and may even cause your computer to 'hang-up' or crash. Some network applications may interfere with each other, if you try to run them at the same time. If you are experiencing problems, try running only one network application at once. In all cases, it is recommended that you get your LAN system manager to install network applications.

Chapter 4

USING REMOTE COMPUTERS

This chapter explains two very basic methods of using remote computers called Telnet and File Transfer Protocol (FTP). Telnet is the program to use if you want to log-in to a remote computer and use that computer as if you were actually sitting at its keyboard. FTP is the program to use if you want to transfer files between computers on a network, such as text documents, graphics files, pictures, games programs, utility programs, etc. FTP is a particularly useful way of exploring the Internet, since there are very many Internet computers that you can access by this method. These facilities are available on most LANs and BBSs. They can be used within your LAN or to use the resources of many other computers connected to the Internet. Even if you do not have FTP capability on your computer, you can still get files from some FTP archives on the Internet by sending electronic mail messages to the automatic mail server, as described in Chapter 5.

Telnet and FTP have both been around for many years and are quite basic, but they are still very useful and powerful tools. Another important tool is the Archie program, which is especially useful for finding files that you want to retrieve by FTP. Archie, along with more sophisticated ways of exploring networks and accessing information archives, such as WAIS, Gopher and World Wide Web, are described in Chapter 7.

Computer Names
In order to access another computer on a network, using FTP or Telnet, it is useful to understand how computers

are named. Furthermore, computer names are used when addressing electronic mail, as described in Chapter 5.

Networked computers always have a name and a number code, so that they can be identified by the server, other users of the network, and possibly the Internet too. Computers connected to the Internet are often called hosts, and these computers will always have an Internet Protocol (IP) host name and number. The host names are constructed using a hierarchical system called the Domain Name System (DNS). The host name usually consists of 2-5 short alphabetic codes separated by full-stops ('periods' in American English), and is usually typed in lower case letters. These full-stops are commonly referred to as 'dots', so that the name *vuw.ac.nz* is said 'vuw dot ac dot nz'.

The codes are nearly always written in the same order, except sometimes in the UK, where some mail programs use the old British convention for host names, in which the name is written in reverse order. For example, instead of *glg.ed.ac.uk*, the name becomes *uk.ac.ed.glg*. If friends overseas are having problems e-mailing you in the UK, it may be worth them trying a reverse-ordered address.

The last part of the host name is usually the country code, although this is normally omitted for hosts in the USA. For example, for the host *src.doc.ic.ac.uk*, the country code is *uk*. There are two-letter codes assigned for most countries in the World. Some common ones you will come across are: *au* = Australia, *br* = Brazil, *ca* = Canada, *fi* = Finland, *fr* = France, *jp* = Japan, *il* = Israel, *nl* = The Netherlands, *no* = Norway, *nz* = New Zealand, *es* = Spain, *se* = Sweden, *ch* = Switzerland, and *us* = USA. The country code part of the host name is also known as the 'zone'.

In the USA, the last part of the host name normally refers to the type of organisation that the host serves. For example, for the host *wuarchive.wustl.edu*, the type is *edu*, short for education. This is also called the 'zone'. There are a number of other three-letter zone codes that you will come across: *com* = commercial organisation, *gov* = government, *int* = international organisation (mostly NATO), *mil* = military, *net* = networking organisation, *org* = any non-commercial organisation. You may also come across some other rarer zone codes that refer to non-Internet networks that are linked to the Internet by gateways, such as: *bitnet* =a zone that covers all users of the BITNET network service, and *uucp* = the UUCP network for users of Unix computers.

Outside of the USA, the code to the left of the zone gives the type of organisation. For example, for the host *src.doc.ic.ac.uk*, the type of organisation is *ac*, short for academic. Thus *ac* is the equivalent of *edu* in the USA. You will come across a wide variety of other codes, similar to the ones listed for the USA above, that denote the organisation type. For example, *co* means commercial, and *org* means any miscellaneous organisation.

The next code to the left of the organisation type code is usually an abbreviation of the organisation's name. For example, for the host *src.doc.ic.ac.uk*, the *ic* stands for Imperial College, which is in London.

To the left again, there may be one or two more codes, which refer to the particular computer or LAN that is connected to the Internet. There may be more than one computer or LAN connected at a given site. For example, at Edinburgh University, there are two mainframe computers called Festival and Castle, and their respective host names are *festival.ed.ac.uk* and *castle.ed.ac.uk*. There are also several LANs connected to the Internet at

Edinburgh University. The Department of Geology and Geophysics has a LAN that is called *glg*, and has the Internet host name *glg.ed.ac.uk.*

Within one LAN, or within a local collection of LANs and networked mainframes, which is often called a 'domain', it is not usually necessary to use the full IP host name. For example, within the Edinburgh University domain, which is *ed.ac.uk*, the Castle and Festival computers can normally be identified simply as *castle* and *festival*. Within the *glg* LAN at Edinburgh University, there are a large number of networked PCs and Macintoshes, all of which have their own names within the *glg* domain, and which happen to be named after flowers, e.g. *poppy*, *daisy*, etc.! Within the *glg* domain, all these computers can be identified simply by their names.

The IP host name system is meant to make it easy for humans to remember the names of hosts. However, network software usually uses a numerical equivalent of the host name, which is called the host number. The host number is usually 4-5 numbers, 1-3 digits each, separated by full-stops. For example, the host number equivalent of *castle.ed.ac.uk* is currently *129.215.128.23*. Note that the numeric domains are in the reverse order to the alphabetic domains, so that in this case, 129 is the number for the UK, and 23 is the number of *castle*. Even Macintoshes and PCs on a LAN will normally have their own host number. Most users will not need to worry too much about host numbers, and should always use the host name where possible. Also, system managers may rearrange a network from time to time, and change the host numbers. However, the host names should not change, unless the system manager informs you otherwise. Occasionally one host may have more than one name, although this is not common. This just means that you can address the host computer by either of its names.

Telnet

There are a number of programs for PCs and Macintoshes that allow Telnet access to other machines, such as the widespread and popular Telnet programs from the National Center for Supercomputing Applications (NCSA), at the University of Illinois. There are also WIMP-based products, such as the PC program *Chameleon* and the Macintosh program *MacIP*. Most LANs have a built-in Telnet facility, so ask your system manager how to start it.

After starting a Telnet program such as NCSA *Telnet*, logging-in to a remote Internet host will usually require you to enter something like *telnet hostname*, where *hostname* is the full IP host name or host number of the remote Internet host (Figure 4.1). Alternatively just type *telnet*, which will give you the *telnet>* prompt, and then type *open hostname*. For example, if I wanted to connect to a computer called Matai, at Victoria University of Wellington, New Zealand, I would type *telnet matai.vuw.ac.nz*, or I would type *telnet* and at the *telnet>* prompt I would type *open matai.vuw.ac.nz*. More sophisticated WIMP-based Telnet programs may just want you to enter the IP host name of the remote computer in a special dialogue box.

Your Telnet program will then attempt to connect you to the remote host computer, which may take only a fraction of a second, or may take a few seconds if the computer is on the other side of the world. Sometimes, the host name may not be recognised and you will get a message such as 'unknown host' or 'host is unreachable'. If this happens, check that you have typed the host name correctly, and in full, using the standard IP format. If this is not the problem, it is possible that the computer you are using to connect to the Internet does not recognise the host name, even though it may actually exist. In this case you can try the host number, if you know it, instead of the host name. If the Internet is very busy, or the remote computer is down for repairs, you may have to try again later. Another possibility is that the remote computer is on a network which can not be reached by the Internet, and therefore you will not be able to use Telnet to connect to it.

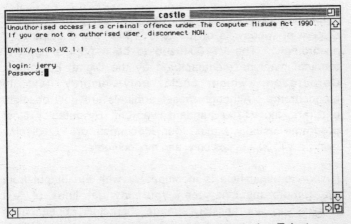

```
════════════════════ castle ════════════════════
Unauthorised access is a criminal offence under The Computer Misuse Act 1990.
If you are not an authorised user, disconnect NOW.

DYNIX/ptx(R) V2.1.1

login: jerry
Password: █
```

Figure 4.1 Logging-in to a remote host using Telnet.

During the process of logging-in to the remote computer, Telnet will normally inform you of the 'escape character', which is the key combination you should press, should you have problems disconnecting from the remote computer. This is commonly *ctrl*-] (i.e. the control key and the right-hand square bracket, pressed at the same time).

Telnet is mostly used by people to remotely access computers for which they already have an account. Thus they will be able to enter their user name and password when prompted to do so. A few computers will allow guest access, although not many. These computers may tell you when you connect to them what user name to enter if you wish to log-in as a guest. Similarly, they may tell you whether a password is necessary for a guest user, and if so, what to enter. Unless you have a legitimate account on the computer that you are connecting to with Telnet, or the computer accepts guest log-ins, then you will not be able to use that computer. If you find you cannot log-in, then use the escape character mentioned above to quit Telnet.

Many remote computers will assume that your computer display or window is of the type 'VT100', and output text accordingly. The VT100 used to be a popular type of terminal machine manufactured by the Digital Equipment Corporation, which could only display text in monochrome. Although these terminals are now obsolete and rare, the VT100 standard lives on. By default, Telnet programs usually make your Macintosh or PC display mimic a VT100, i.e. text only, and monochrome.

If your terminal type is incompatible with the output from the remote machine, then you may get lines of text breaking-up, and possibly strange characters appearing on your screen. There are other terminal types apart from VT100, such as ANSI and 3101, and you will either need to instruct your Telnet program to accept output in the appropriate format, or, instruct the remote computer to output in a format compatible with your Telnet program, such as VT100. This can normally be done by typing 'set term vt100' or similar, at the Telnet prompt.

Once you have logged-in successfully, and you are using the correct terminal type, you are free to explore and use the facilities on the remote computer. If you have logged-in as a guest, your facilities will usually be limited in some way. You will only be able to see and use certain files. If you are a registered user of the remote computer, then you will probably have more freedom to roam from directory to directory, to download files and to use the programs on the computer.

A good way to find out is to experiment and see. Most remote computers that you can connect to over the Internet will be Unix workstations or mainframe computers. Other remote computers may use the VMS operating system instead. So it is worth while becoming acquainted with the basic commands in these two operating systems.

The most useful commands are:

Unix	VMS	Function
cd	*CD*	change to the home directory
cd dir-name	*CD dir-name*	change to a directory named *dir-name*
cd ..	*CD ..*	change to the next higher ranking directory
ls	*DIR*	list the files within the current directory
rm f1	*DEL f1*	removes the file named *f1*
cp f1 f2	*COPY f1 f2*	make a copy of a file called *f1* and call it *f2*
pwd	*SH DEF*	show current directory you are using
man	*HELP*	the on-line help system
man command	*HELP command*	gives information on the specified *command*

Note that VMS is quite similar to DOS for PCs, since DOS was originally developed from VMS.

To log-out from the remote computer, it is usually sufficient to type *logout*, *exit*, *bye*, *quit* or *ctrl*-D (i.e. the control key and 'D' at the same time) at the prompt. If you then find yourself at the *telnet>* prompt, type *quit* to exit the Telnet program. If you are having problems, press the escape key combination that you were given by the remote computer when you logged-in. If you are getting really desperate, simply close the window in which you are working, or quit the Telnet program. Doing either of these things will cause your Telnet program to close down the connection to the remote computer.

Shareware and Freeware

Shareware is software that is widely distributed on non-commercial and commercial computer archives. It is easy to find and you are encouraged to copy and use it, on the understanding that if you like and continue to use the software, you will register your use with the authors, and according to the authors' wishes, either send them a small fee or make a donation to a charity of their choice. Freeware is similar to shareware, except that the authors do not expect any payments to be made, so it really is free.

Freeware and shareware can be acquired by a variety of methods. Many PC and Macintosh oriented computing magazines give away disks containing freeware and shareware, attached to the front covers of the magazines. You can also buy shareware on disks, from various vendors, at very reasonable prices. Major shareware vendors in the UK include Omicron, Red Dragon Software, Shareware Orderline and Testware, amongst others, which may be found advertising in computer magazines. Alternatively, you may use your network and Internet links to obtain shareware and freeware, either via a BBS (see Chapter 1), or by using FTP (described below).

File Transfer Protocol (FTP)

File Transfer Protocol (FTP) is a method for transferring computer data files from one computer to another. These files may be utility programs, games, pictures, text, or virtually anything. FTP is often used to transfer files from larger computers, such as workstations or mainframe computers, onto your PC or Macintosh. This process of transferring files from a large computer to a small computer is often called 'downloading'.

To do this you will need access to an FTP program for DOS, *Windows* or Macintosh. There are several programs to choose from, which are either commercial, shareware or freeware. One of the most basic, but widely used programs that provides FTP facilities, is NCSA *Telnet*, available for Macintoshes and PCs. This is commonly used on LANs and for accessing the Internet via a LAN. Another program, called *Fetch,* provides user-friendly FTP for Macintosh users. If you use a LAN, your LAN system manager will be able to tell you which FTP program is used on your LAN.

There are also programs for use with a BBS. *WigWam* from Ashmount Research is one such program that provides users of the CIX bulletin board with FTP access. *Ameol* from CIX themselves is another. Programs that are not tied to one particular Internet provider are NetManage *Chameleon* and the freeware programs NCSA *Mosaic* and *Cello*. BBS subscribers should contact their BBS company to find out the preferred FTP program.

If you have a Macintosh or *Windows* FTP program, connecting to a remote computer is relatively simple. Firstly you must select the 'connect' option from the menu, and then select the computer you wish to connect to, or enter the IP host name of the computer into a dialogue box. For example, to connect to the FTP site at Imperial College, you would enter *src.doc.ic.ac.uk.*

Alternatively, you may be able to FTP the remote host computer by entering *ftp hostname*, where *hostname* is the IP host name of the computer you want to connect to. You can also enter *ftp* only to start the FTP program, and you will get a prompt *ftp>* after which you should enter *open hostname*, where *hostname* is the IP host name of the remote computer. For example, to connect to Imperial College, London, you can either enter *ftp src.doc.ic.ac.uk* or *ftp* followed by *open src.doc.ic.ac.uk*.

Once FTP contact has been established with the remote computer, it will display the name of the computer you have connected to, and ask you to enter your user name. Unless you already have a user name and password for the computer in question, you can often log-in with the user name 'anonymous', or 'guest'. Many Internet host computers will accept 'anonymous FTP' log-ins, such as those listed at the end of this chapter. If there are too many other people trying to use the computer via anonymous FTP, you will be refused access, in which case you should try again at another time of day (or night) when there may be fewer people on the system. Remember that the computer you are accessing may be in another country, and their peak usage times may not coincide with office hours in your country.

The computer will then ask you to enter a password. If you are using anonymous FTP, you can probably type anything at this stage, and still get access, but it is not recommended. You should type in your full electronic mail address (see Chapter 5 if you do not know what this is), so that the system managers know who is using their computer. If you do not type in your full address, you may find that your access to files is automatically restricted. Note that as you type in your address, it will not be printed on the screen, since the remote computer is treating it as a password. This is normal, so just keep typing and then press *enter* or *return*.

By this stage, you may have found that your computer is reacting very slowly. It is quite normal to get a few seconds pause between entering something, and getting a response. This is because you are competing with many other users of the Internet, possibly over long distance intercontinental cables or satellite links, so you need to be patient. However, if things become impossibly slow, you should try at another time of day when perhaps the Internet will be less busy. Alternatively, try using a computer archive closer to home, which may have what you are looking for.

Once your user name and password have been accepted you will be logged-in. If you are using anonymous FTP you will be welcomed to the computer with some information and instructions about its use. Please read these notes carefully, and do not infringe the rules of the system. Always remember you are a guest on someone else's computer, and you should abide by their rules. Selfish behaviour will only result in the system managers making the computer less accessible, or even making it unavailable to the public.

Once you have logged-in, some Macintosh and *Windows*-based FTP programs will show you all the available directories and files on the Internet host computer as menu items. You can change directories by pressing the appropriate buttons. Alternatively, if you have a less sophisticated FTP program, you will be presented with a prompt for input, usually *ftp>*. You can move from one directory to another, list the contents of directories and download files by entering commands at the prompt. Only a few simple commands will be recognised.

The most important commands are:

ls   list all files and subdirectories in the current
       directory
dir list all files and subdirectories in the current
       directory

ls -l	gives full details of all files and subdirectories in the current directory
cd	change current directory, e.g. *cd /pub/pc* will put you into the specified *pc* directory
cdup	to move back up to a higher ranking directory
cd /	to move back up to the 'login', 'root', or 'top' directory
pwd	this will ask the computer to tell you which directory you are in, should you forget
ascii	select ASCII format before downloading a text or ASCII file
binary	select binary format, for all files other than ASCII files
get	get the file you want, e.g. *get chess.zip* will retrieve the specified chess program
mget	will retrieve more than one file if followed by a list of files or a filename pattern
quit	to log-out when you have finished
bye	to log-out when you have finished

These are all the commands you really need to know, although there are several others. If you want to find out about the other commands you may use, you can type the command *help*. This will produce a list of all the permissible commands on your screen.

You will often need to spend some time exploring an FTP site, by changing directories and then listing all the files in a directory. You may find that some directories are 'mysteriously' empty, particularly if you are logged-in via anonymous FTP. This is because, like any user of a large computer or LAN, what you are privileged to see and use is limited, unless you happen to be the system manager. You will soon get used to spotting directory and file names that might be of interest. Directories called 'pub' and 'packages' usually contain subdirectories and files of interest to Macintosh and PC users. Also, look out for files that contain 'readme' or 'index' in the file name.

These are text files that you can download, and then read using any text editor or word-processor program. They contain useful information and descriptions of the other files at the FTP site. So, rather than randomly downloading files that you hope might be useful to you, and then deleting ones that are not, it is better to read the 'readme' and 'index' files first, to find the files you really want to download.

With some Macintosh and *Windows* FTP programs downloading a file is as simple as selecting the required file from a menu list, selecting the directory on your computer that it is to be transferred to, choosing binary or ASCII transfer format, and then clicking on the download or transfer option. It is important to select which PC directory or Macintosh folder you wish to transfer the file to. If you have not taken care to set this properly, the file may be transferred to a default location, where you might not be able to find it very easily. If this happens, try looking in the folder or directory where your FTP program resides, or use the Macintosh File Find option, or the *Windows* File Manager File Search option, to find the file. Also, be careful that you do not already have a file on your computer, in the selected transfer directory, with the same name as the one you are transferring, since it will be replaced with the transferred file. You will not be able to recover the one that was there before. If this is going to be a problem, your FTP program should have an option to rename a file as it is transferred.

With more primitive FTP programs, to download a single file, enter *get filename* at the FTP prompt, where *filename* is the name of the file that you want. Make sure that you type in the file name exactly as it should be, and make sure the case of the letters is correct, otherwise it will not work. You can also enter *get filename1 filename2*, if you want to rename the original file *filename1* when it is transferred and call it *filename2*.

To get several files, you can enter *mget* (meaning 'multiple get') followed by a list of file names. Alternatively, if all the file names conform to a pattern, then you can use a pattern, containing the 'wild card' symbol, which is an asterisk. For example, entering *mget text** would retrieve all files whose names began with the letters *text*. When using *mget* the computer will ask you whether you want to transfer each file before it actually does so. Press 'y' to transfer, or 'n' to skip it.

Make sure that you are in binary mode when you transfer a file, unless you definitely know that it is an ASCII or text file. Most files are binary files, other than files with names like 'readme' and 'index', and files with *.hqx*, *.txt* or *.doc* extensions. If you download a binary file as an ASCII file by mistake, it will transfer an unusable file to your computer. In order to switch to binary mode, type *binary* at the FTP prompt, at which point the remote computer will display 'Type set to I'. To switch to text mode, type *ascii* at the prompt, to which the remote computer responds 'Type set to A'.

Besides downloading files, you may want to send files from your Internet host computer to the remote computer. This process is the converse of 'downloading', and thus is usually called 'uploading'. To do this, just use *send* (or *put*) instead of the *get* command. Also, you can use *mput*, which, like *mget* allows the transfer of multiple files. You can do this if the remote computer allows anonymous FTP users to contribute files. Also, if you are a registered user of the remote computer, with your own user name and password, then there should be no problem in using FTP to transfer files into your personal home directories on that computer, or to other directories for which you have the appropriate privileges.

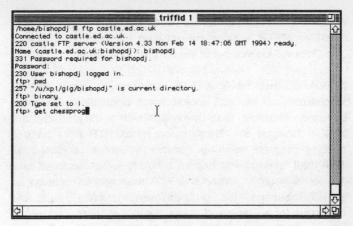

```
                        triffid 1
/home/bishopdj % ftp castle.ed.ac.uk
Connected to castle.ed.ac.uk.
220 castle FTP server (Version 4.33 Mon Feb 14 18:47:06 GMT 1994) ready.
Name (castle.ed.ac.uk:bishopdj): bishopdj
331 Password required for bishopdj.
Password:
230 User bishopdj logged in.
ftp> pwd
257 "/u/xp1/glg/bishopdj" is current directory.
ftp> binary
200 Type set to I.
ftp> get chessprog
```

Figure 4.2 A typical FTP session.

When you use *send* , *put* or *get* , the file is transferred
and you will be informed of progress as the transfer takes
place. Depending on the size of a file, and the distance
that it is being transferred, the time taken may be only a
few seconds, or many minutes. If your transfers are
taking a long time, think about whether you really need
what you are transferring, and whether it might be
possible to obtain it from a site closer to your computer.
If the transfer is very slow indeed, you may wish to
abort the process, by pressing *ctrl*-C (the *ctrl* key and 'C'
at the same time).

The *send, put* and *get* commands also allow you to
rename the file as it is transferred. Simply add the new
file name at the end of the command line, e.g. to rename
chess.zip to *chess2.zip*, you can use the command *get
chess.zip chess2.zip*. Sometimes FTP will not recognise
certain filenames, if they are in a format that is illegal in
Unix (e.g. if they resemble Unix commands). Make sure
you use only legal filenames.

When you have transferred what you want, you should finish your FTP session by entering the command *bye* or *quit*. This will log you out of the remote computer.

If you do not have a FTP program on your PC or Macintosh, you can still access some anonymous FTP sites by using electronic mail (e-mail), which is described more fully in Chapter 5. These anonymous FTP sites have a special program running constantly, which is called an 'FTP mail server' and has an ordinary e-mail address as if it were a person. When the FTP mail server receives an e-mail message, the program automatically reads the message for sense, and takes the appropriate action. In this way you can e-mail a request for a file, and the mail server will automatically send the file back to you by e-mail. There are various ways in which you can e-mail your request, depending on the FTP mail server that you are using. To find out how, it is best to send an e-mail message containing the single word 'help', and you will then get instructions e-mailed to you. FTP mail servers normally expect a list of standard FTP commands in your e-mail message, as described above, with each command on a separate line. Several FTP mail server addresses are listed at the end of this chapter.

File Compression
Once you have located your transferred file on your PC or Macintosh hard disk, you may be able to use it immediately. Files with the extension *.exe* may be executed immediately. Files ending *.txt* or *.doc* may be opened using any text editor or word-processor program, and then read. You will also see other files available on FTP archives, with file extensions *.gif, .bmp* or *.jpg*. These are pictures, that have been stored using different binary file formats, which are respectively called GIF (Graphics Interchange Format), bit-map, and JPEG (a format devised by the Joint Photographic Experts Group).

You can download these graphics files onto Macintoshes or PCs, making sure that you type *binary* before you begin the transfer. You will need a special program to be able to view these files and there are a large number of these programs available. For example, two popular ones for viewing GIF files are *WinGif* for PCs running *Windows*, and *GIFConverter* for Macintoshes. Both these programs are shareware, and are available via anonymous FTP. Occasionally, you may come across the file extension *.ps*, which means that the file is in *PostScript* format, which is a file format recognised by many makes of printer. A file ending *.ps* can therefore be sent directly to a *PostScript* printer.

Many files come in a compressed form, to save on storage space, and to enable faster transfer. Compressed files may also be archived, so that several files are amalgamated into one file. Before you can use such files, they must be decompressed and if necessary, extracted from their archive. To do this there are a number of utility programs available for Macintoshes and PCs, most of which are either shareware or freeware, and available via anonymous FTP. PC decompression programs usually have the file extension *.exe*, which means that they are executable. If they are compressed, then they will automatically decompress or 'explode' when you run them. Macintosh decompression programs are commonly compressed, but will decompress themselves automatically when executed. They usually have the file extension *.sea.* Decompression programs are often available from LAN system managers, from BBS companies and may also be bought.

In principle, PC files and Macintosh files can generally be compressed and archived using the same compression formats. For example, *PKZip* compressed archives may be created for both PC and Macintosh files. Thus, in theory, a file extension *.zip* indicates only that it is a

PKZip compressed archive, not whether it is a Macintosh or a PC file. This is true of most of the major compression formats. However, in practice, Macintosh files are usually compressed in different formats from PC files, can be distinguished by their file extensions, and are decompressed using different utility programs. So, generally speaking, files with the extension *.zip* are PC files.

For a *.zip* file, you will need a decompression program such as *PKUnzip*. You may also come across other file extensions which indicate that the file is probably a PC file, for which you will need the appropriate decompression program. These include *.arc* (needs *Arc* or *PKPak*), *.arj* (needs *Arj*), *.lzh* (needs *LHArc*), *.pak* (needs *Pak*), *.zoo* (needs *Zoo*). Be aware, however, that *.arc* , *.lzh*, and *.zoo* file extensions are sometimes used for compressed Atari computer files, as well as PC files. The *.lha* file extension is commonly used for compressed Amiga computer files. Unix files commonly have *.Z*, *.tar* or *.TAR* near the end of the filename, and thus if you are a PC or Macintosh user, these files are unlikely to be of interest.

Macintosh files can usually be recognised by distinctive file extensions, such as *.hqx* and *.gz*. If there is a *.gz* at the end of the filename, you should miss these letters off when you download using FTP. If you do this, the computer at the FTP site will automatically do the first stage of decompression for you. A BinHex file has *.hqx* at the end of the filename, which denotes that the file has been encoded in an ASCII format that is liable to cause fewer errors on transmission. You may need a special utility program to decode a BinHex file, although Macintosh FTP programs such as *Fetch* will often give you the option to decode the BinHex automatically as the file is downloaded. A program called *BinHex* will also do the job, although it will not do any further decompression that

may be necessary once the BinHex file has been decoded.
More useful utilities are *StuffIt Expander* or *StuffIt Lite*
from Aladdin Systems, which are freeware programs.
Compact Pro will also decode BinHex files, but is
shareware. Sometimes you will also see the file
extension *.bin*, which means that the file has been encoded
using MacBinary format. *Fetch* will automatically decode
a MacBinary file, or you can use *StuffIt Expander*. Once
you have decoded the BinHex or MacBinary file, you will
usually be left with one more stage of decompression to
do. The filename may now have either *.sit* or *.cpt* at the
end. *StuffIt Expander* will decompress both these kinds
of compressed files, whilst *Compact Pro* will only
decompress *.cpt* files. Sometimes you will come across
the file extension *.sea*, mentioned earlier, which stands
for 'self extracting archive'. When you execute this file,
it will decompress itself automatically.

Since e-mail is always sent in ASCII (text) format, files
sent to you by FTP mail servers will be in ASCII format.
Some files may be encoded as BinHex, for which you will
need a special decoding program, as described above.
'Uuencoded' is another format that is sometimes used, and
is also used for downloading files from Network News as
described in Chapter 6. There are several commercial,
shareware and freeware programs available for
Macintoshes and PCs that will allow you to decode a
'uuencoded' file.

When you decompress either a PC or a Macintosh file, it
will usually generate more than one new file or directory.
Look carefully at what you have produced during
decompression, to see which is the executable file (if
any). PC users will recognise the *.exe* file extension
denoting the executable file.

Remember that files transferred by FTP may carry
viruses of the kind described in Chapter 3. Always check

new files that you download with a virus protection utility program to make sure that they are not infected.

Finding Games, Utilities and Pictures

There is now a huge number of computers around the world that can be accessed via anonymous FTP. These computers are usually mainframe computers or workstations using either the Unix or VMS languages. They are located mainly in academic and government institutions. Some of the largest file archives are in the USA. However, it is common practice for system managers at anonymous FTP sites to copy what is available at sites other than their own, creating what are called 'mirrors'. Thus, if you are connected to a British FTP site, you are likely to find 'mirror' directories containing files from FTP sites in the USA and elsewhere. It is much better to download files from a mirror directory at a FTP site in your own country, rather than from the original site in some other country, since it saves you time and stops the Internet from getting overloaded.

It is impossible to list here all the anonymous FTP sites that are available, since there is a huge number, and sites tend to come and go, sometimes within a matter of months. However, some sites have been going for several years and are well-known sources. Ones that you can try include:

ftp.demon.co.uk	UK
src.doc.ic.ac.uk	UK
sumex-aim.stanford.edu	USA
wuarchive.wustl.edu	USA
wsmr-simtel20.army.mil	USA
ftp.sunet.se	Sweden
garbo.uwasa.fi	Finland
nic.funet.fi	Finland

Also, there are a number of FTP mail servers around the world, such as:

bitftp@pucc.princeton.edu   USA
ftpmail@doc.ic.ac.uk   UK
ftpmail@grasp.insa-lyon.fr   France
bitftp@vm.gmd.de   Germany

If you log-in to an FTP site as an 'anonymous' or 'guest' user, you can search directories for the files that you want. Look out for 'mirror' directories, as described above. Directories named 'pub' and 'packages' often contain useful files. 'Index' and 'readme' files also contain useful information. However, searching for files simply by browsing through the directories at anonymous FTP sites can be very time consuming. An easier way to find what you are looking for is to use an Archie service, or to use one of the information server programs, described in Chapter 7.

Chapter 5

ELECTRONIC MAIL

One of the greatest benefits of using a network is the ease with which you can communicate with other people who are connected to that network. It makes no difference whether they are in the same room or on the other side of the world. Not only does it allow you to send messages and files fast, it often costs you nothing. This chapter introduces the basic concepts of electronic mail, and how you can use it. The popular electronic mail programs for Macintoshes and PCs are described, and an outline of the most commonly used functions is given. A relatively new application of electronic mail, sending faxes, is also described. Lastly, in a section on 'E-mail Etiquette', there are hints and tips on how to use this medium effectively.

What is E-mail?
Electronic mail, or 'e-mail', as it is commonly known, is probably the most commonly used feature on any network, including LANs, BBSs, and the Internet. Virtually any computer that is connected to a network is capable of sending and receiving e-mail, to and from other network users, provided it has the appropriate e-mail software installed.

E-mail is sent and received using a mail program, sometimes called a 'mailer'. The sender types a message in at their computer keyboard, using their mail program. A typical e-mail message may only be a few lines, since it is conventional for e-mail messages to be much less wordy and formal than most ordinary letters. Outgoing messages automatically contain the date and sender's address, which allows the sender to get straight on with writing the message. E-mail is so easy to use that people tend to send messages much more frequently than ordinary letters, and hence there is usually less to write. It would not be unusual for someone to send several e-mail messages to the same recipient within one day. However, there is no need to keep messages short, and it is possible to send many pages of text. It is also becoming increasingly common to be able to attach computer files to your message, which might contain graphics, pictures, or other data.

Once an e-mail message has been typed into the mail program, and the recipient's e-mail address has been entered, the message is ready to send. It is usually possible to enter more than one address, if desired, so that the message can be sent simultaneously to different recipients. Often, there is an option to keep a copy of every outgoing message for later reference.

Once e-mail has been sent, it can take anything from a few seconds to a few hours to reach its destination, depending on the distance the message must travel, how many computers it is routed through, and how fast those computers are processing e-mail. Occasionally, a crucial computer link is out of action for a while, in which case an e-mail message may take a day or so. However, this is not very common. Remember that messages sent from other time zones will have the local date and time recorded in the message header. If you make allowances for this you should find that most international e-mail messages actually arrive within a few minutes.

On arrival the e-mail message will be stored by the recipient's mail server computer, until the recipient logs-in, starts up their mail program and can read the message. They can then choose to either keep or destroy the message, or forward it to another person on the network. If they wish to reply to the message, they will normally be able to use the automatic reply facility in their mail program, which looks at the original message to find out where the reply should be sent.

There are many mail programs available for PCs and Macintoshes. However, most of these programs transmit and receive mail using standard protocols for e-mail. These protocols allow different mail programs to understand and communicate with each other. There are currently two main standards for e-mail on PC and Macintosh networks, called SMTP and POP.

Simple Mail Transfer Protocol (SMTP) is a simple network standard for transmission of e-mail messages, and is part of the TCP/IP family of protocols. This is currently the most common protocol used by Macintosh and PC networks and the Internet. SMTP mail programs usually store all e-mail messages on the mail server computer. This means that the messages are quite secure, because they can only be read by the users to whom they belong. However, it does mean that the mail server computer can fill up with users' messages.

Post Office Protocol (POP) is another network standard for transmission of e-mail messages that is gaining popularity. POP mail programs transfer messages from a mail server computer to a user's own computer, thus keeping the mail server from filling up with messages. However, once the messages have been transferred to the Macintosh or PC, they may be read by anyone who has access to that computer, and hence this system is less secure than SMTP. This system also has disadvantages for people who wish to use several different computers to read and write e-mail, since they may end up with their mail scattered across all the computers that they use. To mitigate this problem, some POP mail programs allow you to leave copies of your mail on the mail server, as an SMTP mail program would.

Who can you send E-mail to?

If your computer is connected to a LAN, then you will be able to send messages to anybody using other computers on the LAN. If the LAN is a peer-to-peer network, then the messaging system may be quite rudimentary. If the LAN is a server-based network, then it is more likely that you will have a full e-mail system.

If your LAN is connected to the Internet, then providing your LAN system manager has installed the correct software, it should be possible to send e-mail to anyone else connected to the Internet, i.e. any one of more than 20 million people in 50 countries! You can also e-mail anyone on the Internet if you are connected to the Internet via a modem and a commercial Internet vendor. Many BBSs will also provide you with an e-mail address and the ability to send e-mail to others using the BBS, or anyone connected to the Internet.

Most academic institutions are connected to the Internet, and hence e-mail is a very useful facility for students, teachers and lecturers. A growing number of commercial organisations are also connected, and are making use of e-mail to make major savings in communication costs and time. Now, in some countries you can even send e-mail to people who do not own a computer or who are not connected to a network, but who do have a fax machine. How to send faxes by e-mail is described later in this chapter.

However, some companies, government and military establishments are still reticent about letting their employees have access to the Internet for security reasons. Sending information and computer files by e-mail is so easy that large volumes of confidential data could easily be stolen for private gain. The equivalent of many filing cabinets of documents could be taken, without anyone noticing. One solution would be to censor all outgoing e-mail, but this would be a mammoth task, and instead, many institutions simply do not allow e-mail to be sent out. Institutions also worry about the consequences of computer viruses being imported via e-mail. To prevent this, incoming e-mail may also be prohibited.

E-mail Addresses

You can often find user names of other people on your LAN using your e-mail software. Microsoft *Mail* and Pegasus *Mail* provide this facility (Figure 5.1).

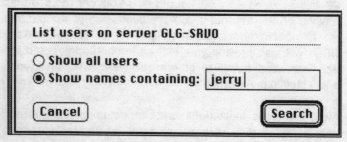

Figure 5.1 Finding a user name on the LAN, using Pegasus Mail on a Macintosh.

If you are sending mail farther afield, then you will need the recipient's full e-mail address. You will need to know the IP host name of the computer, network or BBS where they can read e-mail. You will also need to know their user name. The e-mail address is then usually of the form *username@hostname*. For example, if the full IP host name of my LAN is *glg.ed.ac.uk*, and my user name is *danbishop* then my full e-mail address would be *danbishop@glg.ed.ac.uk*. The part to the left of the @ symbol is often called the mailbox name, so my mailbox name would be *danbishop*. For some Internet users, their mailbox name is not the same as their user name, so make sure you use the correct mailbox name.

When e-mailing other people, or giving other people your e-mail address, make sure you get the address exactly right, or you are likely to have problems. Do not include extra spaces or punctuation, and take care not to interchange lower case letters for upper case letters, or *vice versa*. Valid mailbox names can contain letters, numerals, and punctuation such as full-stops and underscores, but not commas, spaces or brackets. If you really must include these forbidden characters in the mailbox name, then enclose the address in double quotes (" ").

Sometimes you will see a percentage sign in the middle of the mailbox name, e.g. *markus%macs@castle.ed.ac.uk* . In this example, any e-mail sent to this address would initially be sent to the host *castle.ed.ac.uk*. The *castle* computer would then pass it on to *macs*, a server for a Macintosh LAN connected to *castle*. The e-mail message would then be stored on the *macs* server machine until the user *markus* logged-in. So, the percentage sign is just a way of getting the host computer to pass the e-mail message on elsewhere. The e-mail message is said to have 'bounced' off the host machine in question, which in the above example, is called *castle*.

Users of networks other than the Internet will usually have a facility to exchange e-mail with other users, and with users of the Internet. Unfortunately, they often have their own unique system of e-mail addresses, which do not conform to the IP standard, and thus cannot be directly understood by the Internet. For example, CompuServe's addresses comprise two numbers separated by a comma, of the form *xxxxx,yyy*. This is clearly not a standard IP address, so, to enable users outside CompuServe to communicate with CompuServe users, every CompuServe user has a standard IP version of their address, for use with the Internet. The IP e-mail address would be *xxxxx.yyy@compuserve.com* in this case. Note how the comma has been replaced by a full-stop in the mailbox name, because commas are not permitted in the standard IP format for e-mail addresses.

In a similar manner to this, users of many other networks can exchange e-mail with Internet users, by using a standard IP version of their normal network address. For example, BITNET users have the address form *user@host.bitnet* or *user%host.bitnet@gateway* where *user* is their mailbox name, *host* is their host computer name, and *gateway* is the full IP address of a special gateway computer that provides access to BITNET. Similarly, UUCP users have the address form *user@host.uucp* or *user%host.uucp@gateway*. If you are using a network or BBS that has e-mail facilities, but do not know the IP form of your e-mail address, the network administrators or BBS vendor should be able to tell you what it is.

Supposing you know somebody who uses the Internet, but you do not know their e-mail address. The easiest way to find out is to ask them! It seems an old-fashioned approach, but unfortunately there is, as yet, no easy way to find other Internet users' addresses. Another way may be to e-mail a mutual friend or colleague, who may have the address you want. If you have the person's business card, check that. It is becoming increasingly common for people to include their e-mail address on their business cards. Some organisations now produce e-mail directories for their members. Alternatively, you may be able to find out a little by using a Gopher or World Wide Web service, as described in Chapter 7. Some computers that are accessible via Gopher or World Wide Web have a list of personnel at that site, together with e-mail addresses, and possibly postal addresses and telephone numbers. This is particularly common at many academic institutions. These are often called 'white pages directories'. If you know the host name at the site of interest, you may be able to guess at the mailbox name. Try *a.b@hostname* or *a_b@hostname* where *a* and *b* are the first and last names of the intended recipient, since these mailbox formats are common. If this fails, and the message bounces back, you may be able to send the message care of the e-mail systems manager, who will often have the mailbox *postmaster*. So you could try e-mailing *postmaster@hostname*, and ask the system manager to forward a message, or send you the address that you want.

Most mail programs allow the sender to enter two or more recipient addresses, so that the same message may be sent to more than one person. For sending e-mail to larger groups of people, it may be possible to use a 'mailing list', which is a common LAN feature. All users on the mailing list will receive a copy of any message sent to the mailing list address. This is a useful way of broadcasting messages to a group of people who have a common interest. Mailing lists may be maintained automatically by the LAN server machine, or by the system administrator. Contact your system manager to find out how to join or be removed from a mailing list, if you have access to a LAN.

E-mail Headers

Although some e-mail programs do not display them, there are always a number of special lines of text that precede the main e-mail message. These lines are called 'header' lines. The most important header lines are as follows:

Subject:	Subject of the message
To:	Addresses of recipients, separated by commas
Cc:	Addresses of copy recipients, separated by commas (cc = 'carbon copy')

Bcc:	Addresses of 'blind' copy recipients, separated by commas (these recipients will not see who else has received the message)
From:	Address of sender
Reply-To:	Address to reply to
Date:	Time and date sent
Expires:	Date after which message expires
Message-Id:	An identity code for the message generated by the computer
Lines:	The number of lines in the message

The only one of the above header lines that you absolutely must enter into your mail program yourself is the *To:* line. All the others may either be ignored, or will be automatically dealt with by the mail program.

When you receive an e-mail message, you may see some of the header lines described above, but usually not all of them. On some mail programs you can elect to see all of the header lines, in which case you may see some other header lines that are not listed above. Header lines beginning with *Received:* show the path that the e-mail message has taken en-route, i.e. which computers it has been routed through and at what times. Also, other header lines may contain extra information about the origin of the message. Clearly, for the average user, these facts are of limited interest, hence most mail programs do not automatically display them.

What Does it Cost?
Users who are logged-in to a LAN can send e-mail to other LAN users at no cost. For most Internet users at universities and other academic institutions, the use of all e-mail is also free, which is why e-mail is such a popular way for academics to communicate! You will only be liable for some expense if you are using e-mail via a

commercial Internet vendor, or via a BBS. However, using e-mail does not place a great strain on the resources of commercial Internet vendors and BBSs, compared to the other services that they generally offer, and hence the costs of e-mail are usually minimal. Certainly, e-mail charges should be a lot less than sending ordinary mail by post, or faxes, as well as being much quicker.

E-mail Packages
There are a number of shareware and commercial mail programs available for Macintoshes and PCs. Most of these can be used within a LAN and with the Internet, and offer similar facilities. If you are a LAN user, check with your system manager to find out what package he or she thinks is most appropriate for your use. If you are going to use a commercial e-mail service of the type provided by a BBS, then the BBS administrators will recommend an appropriate package to use.

Microsoft *Mail* is a powerful commercially available package, which is ideal for use with either Internet e-mail or e-mail sent within a LAN. It has many functions, although most users may not need them all. Microsoft *Mail* is available for PCs and Macintoshes. Much cheaper options include *Pegasus Mail* and Qualcomm *Eudora*.

Qualcomm *Eudora* is available as a shareware product and also as a fully developed commercial product with extra features. *Eudora* can use the POP mail handling system described earlier in this chapter. It can send enclosures either using BinHex or an important new Internet standard called MIME (Multipurpose Internet Mail Extensions). Applications that comply with MIME can exchange e-mail messages containing images, audio and video. Another mail program, *Mail-It*, also supports MIME.

Pegasus Mail (also known sometimes as *P-Mail*) is an effective and easy to use package for LAN and Internet users, with most of the basic e-mail functions available, including sending enclosures in BinHex format. It is a freeware package, written by David Harris of Dunedin, New Zealand, and is available for DOS, *Windows* and Macintosh users.

Finansa produces a *Windows* e-mail program called *WinMail*. This is primarily for users of a LAN. *Remote WinMail 2* from Finansa is a *Windows* package that will allow you to send and receive e-mail via a modem, as well as a LAN. It can be used to connect to CompuServe, IBM Mail Exchange and the BT Mailbox service, for example. Any of these can then be used to access a wide range of mail services, such as the Internet and proprietary networks such as AT&T, Sprint, Tymnet and MCI Mail.

Basic Functions of E-mail

Normally, when you wish to send an e-mail message, you must firstly enter the e-mail address of the recipient or select the e-mail address from a file of addresses that you have previously entered. The e-mail addresses of your common correspondents can normally be stored in a special file for your convenience, by the e-mail program. This file is often called an 'address book', or in the case of *Eudora*, 'nicknames'. The file contains a list of names and corresponding e-mail addresses, which may be added-to and edited at any time. Keeping an address book allows you to send e-mail more quickly, since you merely select the e-mail address from a list, rather than by typing it in every time (Figure 5.2). Besides saving time, the address book also reduces the number of returned messages by preventing typing errors. It is particularly useful for writing to people who have very long and complex e-mail addresses.

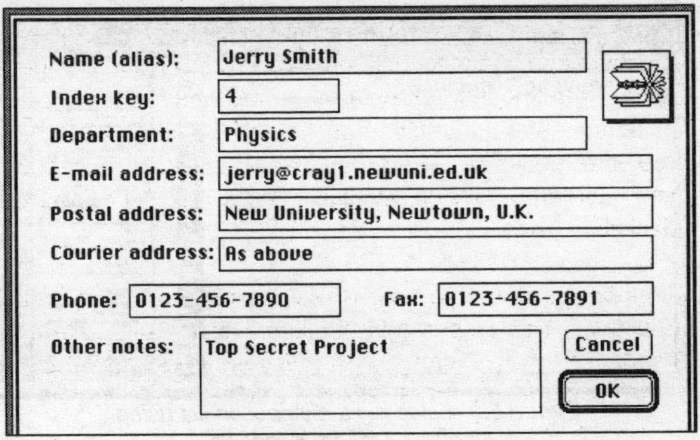

Figure 5.2 The Pegasus Mail address book, on a Macintosh.

You can send copies of your e-mail message to more than one recipient by entering their addresses in the *To:* , *Cc:* or *Bcc:* boxes in the header. If you have more than one address in a box, make sure you separate them with commas. The *To:* box is for the main recipient, and the *Cc:* box is for all other recipients. If you want to send a copy of the message to someone, but do not want them to be able to read in the e-mail header that you have sent copies elsewhere, then enter their address in the *Bcc*: box. If you regularly send your messages to the same group of people, then you may wish to use your e-mail program to create a distribution list (Figure 5.3), which you can then select.

An e-mail message can usually either be written using the e-mail package's own text editor, or written using a word-processing package, copied to the Macintosh or *Windows* 'clipboard' and then 'pasted' into the e-mail package editor. Some e-mail editors are easier to use than others, and some people find it easier to use a word-processing package instead.

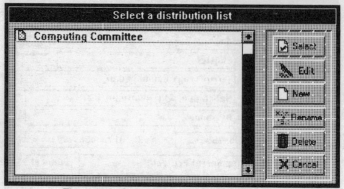

*Figure 5.3 Selecting a distribution list using
Pegasus Mail for Windows.*

However, e-mail messages will usually lose most
formatting when they are transmitted, except for
carriage-returns, so there is absolutely no point in
creating complex formatting and fonts with a word-
processing package, since these will all be lost. If you
need to send a formatted document, then save the
document as a file and send the file as an enclosure, as
described later in this section.

Once the message has been written, it can be sent
immediately, normally by selecting the 'send' button or
menu option (Figure 5.4). Most packages provide the
ability to request a receipt at the time an e-mail message
is sent, so that when the message is received, a receipt
message is automatically generated and returned to the
sender.

In addition, it may be possible to request a message be
sent when the e-mail is actually read by the recipient
(Figure 5.5). Again, if sender and recipient are using
different e-mail packages, then this facility may not
always work. Sometimes the receipts are redirected to
the system manager at either the sender's or recipient's

sites. The system manager may then e-mail the sender, and should be able to help solve this problem.

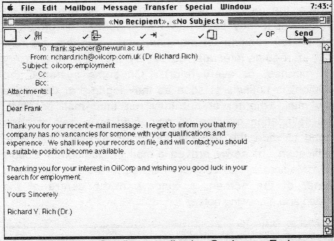

Figure 5.4 *Sending e-mail using Qualcomm Eudora on a Macintosh.*

Message 1	
To:	jerry@cray1.newuni.ac.uk
Subject:	Top Secret
CC:	Col_Saunders@center1.mil
BCC:	
Reply-to:	bishopdj@glg.ed.ac.uk

☒ **Keep a copy of the message**
☐ **Encrypt the message**   **Key:** [   ]
☒ **Request confirmation of reading**
☒ **Request confirmation of delivery**
☒ **Message is urgent**
☒ **Don't add signature when sending**

[Edit message] [Attachments...]   [Send] [Cancel]

Figure 5.5 *Options when sending an e-mail, using Pegasus Mail on a Macintosh.*

When a mail message arrives on the recipient's mail server computer, it is stored there until the recipient logs-in to the system. Depending on the particular system, the recipient may have to run their mail program to find out if they have new mail. Some mail programs can be left running all the time, and will check for new mail at regular intervals, as set by the user (e.g. every ten minutes, or every hour). On some systems, the recipient is notified as soon as they log-in that they have new mail, whether or not they run their mail program. The notification may be accompanied by a bell or other sound to alert the recipient (Figure 5.6). For example, notification of newly arrived e-mail in Qualcomm *Eudora* on a Macintosh can consist of a flag in the top right-hand corner of the screen, a window in the centre of the screen and a crowing noise.

Figure 5.6 The arrival of e-mail in Qualcomm Eudora.

The newly arrived e-mail message may be read immediately, or may be kept and read later (Figure 5.7). Most packages also allow the user to keep copies of both incoming and outgoing messages in special folders or directories, called 'mail folders', or 'In' and 'Out' folders (Figure 5.8). Saved messages should periodically be deleted, especially older messages, to save wasting precious hard disk space. Mail messages with enclosures are especially large and should be deleted as soon as possible.

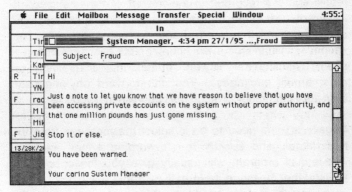

Figure 5.7 Reading e-mail with Qualcomm Eudora on a Macintosh.

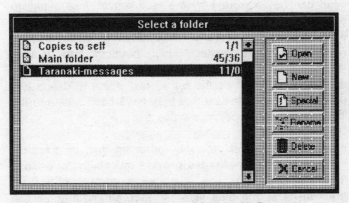

Figure 5.8 Selecting a mail folder with Pegasus Mail for Windows.

Mail folders provide another way of sending messages without typing in the full name of the recipient. The way to do this is to 'reply' to a previous message from the intended recipient. Usually this is simply a case of selecting their e-mail message from the mail folder and then selecting the 'reply' option in your e-mail program. Sometimes this method does not work, often because the return address recorded in the header of their message is incorrect. If this happens, then your message will eventually be 'bounced' back to you, within a few seconds, minutes or even hours. You can try sending it again by using the 'forward' option, that is available on most e-mail packages. You can forward any message from your mail folder to any e-mail address that you like.

Usually, all you need to do is select the message from the mail folder, and specify the forwarding e-mail address. The e-mail program will usually give you the opportunity to edit the message before it is sent, using the e-mail program's built-in text editor. This provides a way for you to forward interesting or witty messages to those who might be interested. Obviously, any e-mail that you send can be forwarded by the recipient of your e-mail to other e-mail users, so always be careful that what you write is not too personal or potentially embarrassing! Also, if you get a message which 'bounces' back to you, you can amend and, hopefully, correct the address before sending it again. Use the e-mail text editor to delete any unnecessary header data that may have been added to the 'bounced' message, before sending it.

If you need to send precisely formatted text, or graphics, then most e-mail packages provide the ability to enclose files with your message, such as word-processor files, graphics files, and data files. In fact, almost any file can normally be sent as an 'enclosure' or 'attachment' (Figure 5.9). BinHex and MIME are the common formats used by e-mail packages for sending enclosures. In addition, it will help your enclosure to be transmitted faster if you make sure the file is firstly reduced in size by using a file compression program, such as one of those mentioned in Chapter 4.

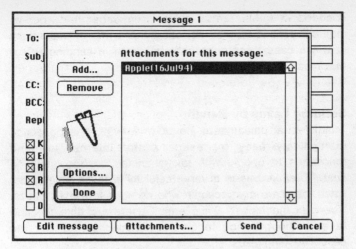

Figure 5.9 Selecting an 'attachment' for an e-mail message, using Pegasus Mail on a Macintosh.

When the enclosure is received by the recipient's e-mail program, their e-mail program should give them the option to decode the BinHex or MIME code and save the decoded file onto their hard disk. If the enclosure was compressed prior to sending, then the recipient needs the appropriate software to decompress the file. If the recipient does not have the appropriate decompression utility program, then it would be better to send the file as a 'self-extracting archive', which means that the file will automatically decompress itself when executed. The recipient of the enclosure will also need software capable of reading and displaying the file, such as a copy of the software package used by the sender to create the file.

However, be warned that sending enclosures may not always work when the sender and the recipient are not running the same e-mail package. There are still some incompatibility problems. For example, not all e-mail packages are capable of decoding enclosures that are encoded in MIME format. Also, remember that your e-mail correspondent may not use either a PC or Macintosh, in which case there is probably no point in sending PC or Macintosh files as enclosures.

Sending Faxes by E-mail

Thanks to an initiative in the USA in 1993, it is becoming increasingly easy for users of the Internet to send messages to people with fax machines, at absolutely no cost. Clearly, this is a very useful thing to be able to do, since there are many people who do not use e-mail, but do have fax machines. Thus e-mail users are able to send faxes without having to own a fax machine or pay the cost of sending faxes.

The method relies on the fact that internal phone calls are free within universities and other institutions, and also local calls are free in some countries. It is also necessary that a computer is especially set up as a fax-server in the free-call area. An e-mail message can then be relayed to the fax-server, which phones the destination fax number and sends the e-mail message as a fax, complete with header sheet. The fax-server then automatically generates a message confirming that the fax was sent successfully, and sends this as an e-mail back to the original sender. If the fax-server was unable to reach the destination fax machine, perhaps because it was engaged, then the fax-server will try again later. If the fax-server cannot send the message, perhaps because the wrong fax number was entered by the sender, then the fax-server computer will eventually abort the operation and send an e-mail message explaining the problem to the original sender.

The number of areas that can be faxed using this method is increasing all the time. It already includes a large number of university sites around the world, the whole of

New Zealand, large parts of the USA and parts of Europe. Only three areas in the UK provide this service at the time of writing, which are the universities of Oxford, Loughborough, and Manchester. Therefore, at present, most fax machines in the UK cannot receive messages via e-mail, but e-mail users in the UK can send messages to fax machines in many places around the world.

A full up-to-date list can be obtained by sending an e-mail message to:

tpc-coverage@town.hall.org

The format of the e-mail address you should use is as follows:

remote-printer.*name*@*faxnumber*.iddd.tpc.int

The *name* can be the name of the person or company, and even their address, which will appear on the cover sheet when the fax is printed out. Use an underscore '_' instead of any spaces, and a slash '/' instead of any carriage returns. For example, the *name*
Joe_Bloggs/Bloggs_Ltd will print out as:

> Please deliver to:
> Joe Bloggs
> Bloggs Ltd

The *faxnumber* should always begin with the country code, followed by the area code and then the actual number. There should be no long distance or international access codes, nor any punctuation. For example, if Joe Bloggs' company is in Wellington, New Zealand, the e-mail address may look something like this:

remote-printer.Joe_Bloggs/Bloggs_Ltd
                    @6441234567.iddd.tpc.int

The first two digits of the number are 64, which is the country code for New Zealand, and the following digit 4 is the area code for the city of Wellington. The last seven digits represent any fax number.

More information about this service can be requested by sending an e-mail to:

tpc-faq@town.hall.org

Questions about how to set up a fax-server in your area, and other administrative questions should be sent to:

tpc-admin@town.hall.org

E-mail Etiquette

E-mail messages are rarely as formal in style and content as letters. It is almost unknown to start a message with the salutation 'Dear Sir' or 'Dear Madam'. Usually 'Dear Fred', 'Fred', 'Hello', or 'Hi' will do, depending on how well you know the person concerned. Instead of signing off with 'Yours Sincerely' or similar, it is more usual to finish more casually, with 'Regards', 'Best Wishes' or similar. Many people create a standard signature using their e-mail program, which is then automatically appended to every message that they send. Signatures should be short, no more than 4 or 5 lines at most, and should include useful information such as your full name, organisation, postal address, telephone number, fax number and e-mail address. The latter is often useful should the return-address in the header of your out-going message get scrambled, or cannot be correctly read by the reply facility of your correspondent's e-mail program. Some people create very fancy signatures, including stylised pictures and quotes, which vary from being witty, to being obscure or pretentious. These are not really necessary, and are liable to become an irritation to your regular correspondents.

On most networks, e-mail is not highly regulated, if at all, since the Internet is so huge and so international that it would be almost impossible to set up any regulatory or censory body. In many ways, this is a good thing, providing unlimited freedom of speech. However, it is also a freedom that is easy to abuse, and abuse is not unknown. Unfortunately there are a few unpleasant characters 'roaming' the Internet. So, although the following points are mostly common sense, they are worth mentioning, since they are clearly not obvious to everyone!

Sometimes e-mail messages are so short and to-the-point that they can be interpreted as being a bit abrupt or rude in tone. So do be careful, especially when writing to people you do not know well! It is easy to unwittingly upset someone.

Be careful with humorous remarks, particularly irony and sarcasm. Without the benefit of hearing your tone of voice, or seeing your facial expression, the recipient may not realise that what you wrote was in jest. At best they may just not understand what you meant, or at worst they may be badly offended. It is common for e-mail writers to use a 'smiley', like this one   :-)   to make it clear that humour was intended (if you do not understand the 'smiley' concept, try turning this page 90 degrees clockwise!).

Do not send messages that might cause you or any other person embarrassment. Furthermore, never send abusive or pointlessly argumentative messages to people, however much you may feel it is warranted. As well as being ill-mannered, it can back-fire badly on you. Remember that e-mail is not particularly private. If you inadvertently enter the wrong address, or make a mistake in the address, or some failure occurs within the e-mail system, your message may be delivered to the wrong person, such as your system manager. You could end-up in a very embarrassing situation. Worse still, you may have your e-mail facility withdrawn by your system manager or BBS, or even worse, you could lose your job!

Do not pass on chain letters. There are a number of these letters circulating on the Internet, which pretend to offer get-rich-quick schemes. Not only are these schemes illegal, they do not work. Furthermore, you are likely to offend those people to whom you send them, and they may think less of you for doing so.

Do not be tempted to over-use mailing lists either. This is a particularly common problem on LANs. Make sure that all the intended recipients are likely to be interested in what you are sending out, otherwise they may regard your messages as 'junk' mail. If you get into the habit of over-using mailing lists and sending 'junk' mail, then your recipients may get into the habit of simply deleting your messages without even bothering to read them! In this way, they could miss relevant messages, and you may find it difficult to communicate with them, even when it is important.

Keep your mail folders tidy, removing old and unwanted messages, and particularly messages with enclosures. This helps to conserve hard-disk space, either on your computer, if your mail program uses POP, or on the mail server computer, if your mail program uses SMTP. Keeping the mail server computer from overflowing with your old e-mail messages will keep your system manager happy too!

Chapter 6

NETWORK NEWS

For those of you wondering if there is more to the Internet than connecting to other computers, moving files around and sending electronic mail to friends and colleagues, there is! The Internet is a melting pot of humanity, as you will find out if you try using Network News! Network News is an electronic forum for discussion on every imaginable topic, and involves millions of people world wide. There truly is something for everyone! In this chapter we describe what Network News is and how to use it. The mostly commonly used programs used to read Network News are described in detail. We also provide some advice on how to 'make friends and influence people' in the Network News fraternity!

What is Network News?

Network News, or 'Net News' for short, is a world wide bulletin board and conferencing system also known as 'Usenet', short for 'users' network'. Although Usenet is closely related to the Internet, it is not the same thing. However, most Internet and BBS users are able to access Usenet. Since Network News is not owned by any person or organisation, it is largely unregulated and uncensored. It is run by volunteers around the world, and is supported by the millions of users of the Internet and other networks. Furthermore, Network News is absolutely free, although you will still have to pay any Internet access fees, if you normally have to do so.

The news system allows users to enter messages that may then be read by thousands or even millions of other users, either within their local area, within their country, or all around the world. Messages are always sent to a 'newsgroup', which has a name and a common theme, e.g. gardening, TV shows, cars, etc (Figure 6.1). Messages sent to newsgroups are usually called 'articles', and the process of placing an article in a newsgroup is called 'posting'. Users can also respond to any messages if they wish, either by sending a 'follow-up' message, or by sending e-mail to the original sender. A succession of 'follow-up' articles, all on the same subject, is called a 'thread'.

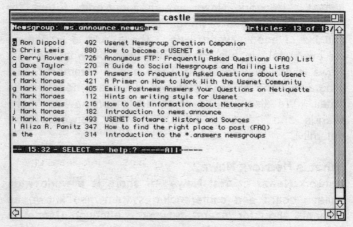

Figure 6.1 A typical selection of articles in a newsgroup.

Some newsgroups are 'moderated' by volunteers, usually those who set up the newsgroup in the first place. When articles are submitted to the moderated newsgroups, they are firstly read by the moderator, who will then post the article, providing it is appropriate to the newsgroup, is reasonably interesting, and does not break any of the standards or rules of the newsgroup. Sometimes moderators may see fit to edit long articles, or articles that may be offensive. Clearly this is a form of censorship, but in practice this means that the quality of the articles is generally higher than in unmoderated groups. Also, there are plenty of unmoderated newsgroups for those who dislike the idea of any kind of censorship.

There are now more than 5,000 newsgroups (and increasing rapidly all the time), and it has been estimated that over 30,000 articles are posted every day, so it is important to be reasonably selective about which newsgroups you wish to read on a regular basis, i.e. subscribe to.

Newsgroups are arranged in a hierarchical system. The most common top-level hierarchies are *alt*, *comp*, *misc*, *news*, *rec*, *sci*, *soc*, and *talk*. These cover a huge variety of topics, as described below:

alt   An unofficial hierarchy of 'alternative' newsgroups, that covers a vast range of topics which are generally not covered in the official hierarchies. The newsgroups in this hierarchy tend to appear and disappear quite quickly.

comp   Covers all discussion of computer related topics.

misc   Covers a miscellany of topics.

news   Provides news and information about Network News itself.

rec   Covers all types of recreational activities, such as sports, games, arts, etc.

soc   These are a collection of social groups, where discussion can take place between people with mutual social interests.

talk   Mainly for debates and discussion. These groups
         tend to be rather political in content.

Newsgroups within these categories are distributed to
nearly all Internet newsgroup sites world wide, although
some of the 'alt' newsgroups are not carried at many
newsgroup sites.   Also, within your country, town or
institution, there are often newsgroups of local interest.
For example, at Edinburgh University, there is a
hierarchy called *eduni*.

Newsgroups are named depending on their position within
a newsgroup hierarchy.   For example, there are two
newsgroups, whose full names are *rec.games.bridge* and
rec.games.chess.   Both these newsgroups belong to the
games sub-hierarchy of the *rec* hierarchy.   There are
other newsgroups within *rec*, however, such as
rec.food.veg, for example.   Some newsgroup names can be
very long, if they are near the bottom of a hierarchy, e.g.
comp.sys.ibm.pc.hardware.storage.   Newsgroups with
long names tend to be of specialist interest.   The parts of
the newsgroup name are always separated by full-stops.

Look out for the abbreviation *.d*, which stands for
'discussion'.   For example, *rec.humor* is a newsgroup for
those who want to post and read jokes, whereas
rec.humor.d is a newsgroup for those who want to discuss
humour.   There is a subtle difference that should be
observed by posters, if they are not to be rebuked by
other Network News readers.

If you are new to Network News, and have never posted
an article before, you may like to send a test article to
one of the *.test* newsgroups, to see if your system is
working.   When you post such an article, you may get e-
mail messages sent to you automatically by remote
network computers, telling you that your test article has
been received.   Once you are satisfied that you know how

to post articles, you can then compose a proper article and submit it to the relevant newsgroup.

Sometimes it is easy to guess what a newsgroup may be about, just by looking at its name. However, some newsgroup names are a little confusing, misleading or virtually meaningless, particularly within the *alt* hierarchy. The best way to find out what a newsgroup is about is to subscribe to it and read the articles that have been posted. It is always possible to un-subscribe later, if the topics discussed in the newsgroup are not of interest.

Articles posted to a newsgroup do not stay there for ever, otherwise Network News would have become terminally congested many years ago! Many articles are set to time-out when they are posted, i.e. they are marked so they will be deleted after a specified time. Most sites where Network News is received automatically delete all articles that are more than a few weeks old, simply to conserve storage space. Articles in some newsgroups may last longer than others, depending on how much usage those newsgroups get.

As well as the actual message, articles always contain a header, with information about the source of the message. The program used to read newsgroup articles will show some of the header information at the top of each article. At the top of the article there is some information, including the name of the newsgroup, the article number, the name and e-mail address of the sender, the affiliation of the sender (company, university, etc.) and the subject of the article.

For more detailed information and discussion about what Network News is, and what it is not, it is worth having a look at the newsgroup *news.announce.newusers*.

Access to Network News

To be able to read Network News, your PC or Macintosh must be connected to a host computer that can disseminate Network News. Such a computer is often called a 'news feed'. Users of LANs in academic and commercial environments may be able to connect to a news feed computer via their LAN, using a program such as Telnet. Ask your LAN system manager which computer provides your local 'news feed'. Alternatively, you may connect your PC or Macintosh to a BBS news feed by using a modem and the phone. Another option is UUNET, a network that is well known in the USA for providing access to Network News.

Usually, 'news feeds' only carry a limited selection of newsgroups, including ones of local and international interest. The news manager at each site usually has arbitrary and total control over which newsgroups are carried, but is generally open to suggestions. Site news managers provide one of the main forms of control and censorship of Network News.

News feeds tend to be large Unix machines, such as workstations and mainframes, rather than PCs or Macintoshes. Therefore the most popular programs used to access Network News are Unix programs, which are not particularly user friendly in comparison to most *Windows* and Macintosh programs.

News Readers

Three common programs for accessing Network News are *Tass*, *rn* and the *nn* suite of programs. These programs are called 'news reader' programs. Although all three are written for Unix-based computers, PC and Macintosh users are likely to use them when they log-in to the computer that provides their news feed.

When you start using Network News, you will have to decide which of the newsgroups available at your site you wish to subscribe to. Details about which newsgroups you are subscribed to, and which you are not, are usually kept in a file called *.newsrc* on a Unix computer. This file is constantly updated by the news reader program. At first, you may be subscribed to all the available newsgroups at your site, automatically. You will then have to use your news reader program to selectively un-subscribe to newsgroups in which you have no interest. This may be a time consuming process, but providing you do not accidentally delete your *.newsrc* file, you will only have to do it once.

Tass

This is a relatively user friendly Unix news reader program. When you run the program, it presents you with a menu of all the newsgroups you are subscribed to. Against any newsgroups that you have previously read is a number, which refers to the number of articles in that newsgroup. This list of newsgroups may run to several pages. You can move up and down the list, which is in numerical order, either by entering the number next to the newsgroup name, or by using the cursor keys. To open a newsgroup, press the *return* key.

Once you have opened a newsgroup, you are presented with a menu showing all the articles currently available in that newsgroup (Figure 6.2). All articles that you have not read are marked with a cross. Again, you can move up and down the list, either by entering the number of the article, or by using the cursor keys. To read the article, press *return*. The article will then be displayed on your screen.

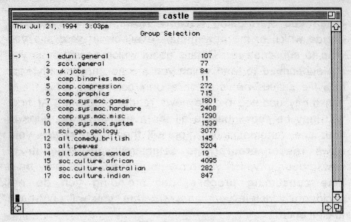

Figure 6.2 The Tass newsgroup menu.

When you are reading an article (Figure 6.3), you may find that there is more than one page, in which case, press the 'space bar' every time you wish to move to the next page. There may be follow-up articles to the one you are reading.

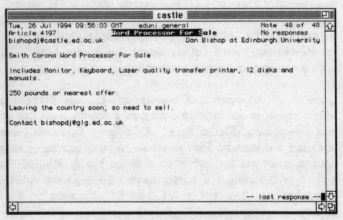

Figure 6.3 Reading news using Tass.

Keep pressing the 'space bar' to read the article and any follow-up articles. Alternatively, you may press *return* to move to the next article or follow-up article, or you may press *tab*, to move on to the next unread article or follow-up article.

To return from reading articles to the menu of articles within the chosen newsgroup, press 'i'. To return to the main menu showing all the available newsgroups, press 't'.

You may wish to un-subscribe from particular newsgroups. To do this, select the newsgroup and then type 'u'. Next time you use the program, this newsgroup will not appear on the main menu. To subscribe to a new newsgroup, type 'y' from the main menu. This will display a menu of all the newsgroups carried by your news feed. You can move up and down the list and select newsgroups as described above. You can also select a newsgroup that you wish to subscribe to, by selecting the newsgroup in question, and typing 's'.

You can also post an article to a newsgroup, firstly by opening the newsgroup, and then by entering 'w'. You will then be prompted for the subject of your message. *Tass* will then run your chosen Unix text editor (your system administrator should be able to show you how to select a default text editor, should you not have a suitable one). Type in your article using the text editor, and then exit the editor. You will then be given the opportunity to post your article. Note that it may take several minutes or hours before the article appears in the newsgroup.

When you have finished using *Tass*, enter 'q' to finish. There are many other commands available in *Tass*, too numerous to mention here. To see a full list of all the available commands, press 'h' from one of the *Tass* menus.

rn

rn is another Unix-based news reader program, probably in more widespread usage than *Tass* , and a little more powerful, although less easy to use. A slightly more powerful version of *rn* is also available, called *trn*.

The first time you run *rn*, it will go through all the available newsgroups at your site, and for each one it will ask you whether you wish to subscribe or not. Also, if some new newsgroups have appeared since you last used *rn*, it will ask you whether you want to subscribe to these too. After each question, answer 'y' or 'n'. It will ask you where you want to put the newsgroups. Press '$' to put the newsgroup at the end of your list of newsgroups, or press '+' followed by the name of an existing group to put it after that group.

Once you have decided which newsgroups you wish to subscribe to, you are then given the opportunity to read each newsgroup, starting with the first on the list (Figure 6.4).

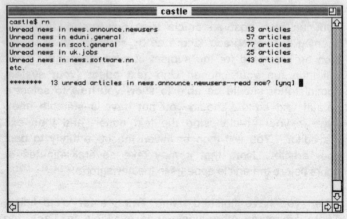

```
                              castle
castle$ rn
Unread news in news.announce.newusers              13 articles
Unread news in eduni.general                       57 articles
Unread news in scot.general                        77 articles
Unread news in uk.jobs                             25 articles
Unread news in news.software.nn                    43 articles
etc.

********  13 unread articles in news.announce.newusers--read now? [ynq] █
```

Figure 6.4 Selecting a newsgroup to read using rn.

To read the suggested newsgroup, answer 'y'. If you wish to move on to the next newsgroup on the list, answer 'n'. When you wish to quit the program, enter 'q'. To go to another newsgroup, enter 'g' followed by the name of the newsgroup. If you are not already subscribed to the newsgroup specified, you will be asked if you want to subscribe first.

When reading a newsgroup, you will always begin with the first article in the newsgroup. If the article is more than one page, you can use the 'space bar' to scroll through the article. Press 'n' to move to the next article, and 'p' to move to the previous article. Type 'q' to finish reading that particular newsgroup. Whilst reading an article, you may enter 's' to save the contents of an article into a file on disk. Enter 'u' to un-subscribe from the newsgroup. Pressing 'r' will allow you to reply to the sender of the article by e-mail. When you enter 'r', the program will automatically transfer you to the default text editor program, allow you to type in your e-mail message, send it, and then return to reading news. Enter 'f' to post a follow-up article for the one you are reading. When you enter 'f', the program will automatically transfer you to the default text editor program, allow you to type in your article, post it, and then return to reading news.

Whilst reading articles in a newsgroup, it is useful to be able to skip articles whose subject is of no interest. When you come across an article that is of no interest, and you wish to skip any follow-ups, press 'k' (lower case). To avoid reading any articles in the future with this subject heading, press 'K' (upper case). To skip the rest of the thread, even if the subject line changes, press 'J' (upper case).

Some articles contain encoded binary files, such as pictures or programs, that you might want to use on your Macintosh or PC. The commonest code is called 'uuencoded' format. The *rn* program is able to decode these automatically. Firstly display the relevant article in *rn*, and then enter 'e' followed by the name of the directory where you want to put the decoded file. If the file is large and is split between more than one article, just repeat this process for each article, making sure that you decode them in the correct order (usually the order in which the articles were posted). You will then have to download your decoded file on to your PC or Macintosh using some other network utility program, such as an FTP (see Chapter 4). There are also commercial, shareware and freeware programs available for PCs and Macintoshes that are able to decode 'uuencoded' files.

There are many other commands available in *rn*. To see a full list of all the available commands, press 'h'.

nn

There is also a suite of Unix news reader programs that go under the name of *nn*, including *nngrep*, *nngrab*, and *nnpost*.

nngrep allows you to find out which newsgroups you are currently subscribed to. If you type *nngrep name,* where *name* is the whole or partial name of the newsgroup, nngrep will list all newsgroups you are currently subscribed to that can be matched with that name. If no name is specified, all the subscribed groups will be listed. Using *nngrep -a name* will list both subscribed and un-subscribed groups. Using *nngrep -u name* lists only un-subscribed groups.

If you wish to read a particular newsgroup, and know its name, you should enter *nn newsgroup*, where *newsgroup* is the name of the newsgroup. If you wish to read all articles on a particular subject, no matter which newsgroup they may appear in, then you should type *nngrab keyword*. The program will then search through the newsgroups you have subscribed to for articles containing the keyword in the subject or keyword line of the article header. This may take a few minutes, but when the search is completed, all relevant articles will be presented for reading.

Typing either *nn* or *nngrab* will cause the *nn* news reader program to start. *nn* presents you with a list of articles that you may read. To move the cursor up and down the list of articles, press the arrow keys. To move on to the next page on the list, press '>', and to move back a page, press '<'. To select an article, type the code letter to the left of the article. You can select several articles in this way. To read the selected articles, press 'Z' (upper case). To scroll through the articles, press the 'space bar', or press 'n' to move on to the next article. Press 'X' (upper case) to move on to the next newsgroup. Press 's' to save an article as a file, or enter ':decode' if you wish to decode a coded file, such as a uuencoded file. If you wish to post a follow-up article in *nn*, you can press 'F' (upper case).

If you want to send a reply by e-mail, press 'R' (upper case). If you want to e-mail the article to someone else, press 'M' (upper case). All these options will transfer you to the default Unix text editor, so that you can compose your message. When you exit from the editor, you will be given the opportunity to post or mail your message, before returning to reading articles. Alternatively, you can post an article without entering the news reader program, by using the program *nnpost*. After typing *nnpost* at the Unix prompt, you will be asked to enter the name of the newsgroups you wish to post to, the subject line, and keywords. You can separate the list of newsgroups and keywords with commas. Then you will be transferred to the editor, as described above (Figure 6.5).

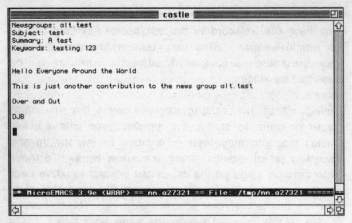

*Figure 6.5 Posting an article using nnpost and
the MicroEMACs text editor.*

Full instructions covering the large number of other
functions available with *nn* are displayed by pressing '?'
whilst running *nn* . To quit using *nn* , press 'Q' (upper
case).

Network News Etiquette

Basically, the same rules apply to Network News
etiquette as e-mail etiquette, which were outlined in
Chapter 5. Formal salutations are virtually unknown, and
salutations of any kind are barely necessary at all.
People commonly use their newsreader program to create
a signature, of the kind described in Chapter 5. Although
it can be fun to have pictures and witty quotes in your
signature, other people will quickly tire of them if you
make a lot of postings, so keep them as brief as possible.

There are some additional rules that should be followed.
Always make sure your contributions are relevant to the
newsgroups to which you send them. There is nothing
more annoying for readers of newsgroups than having to

wade through masses of irrelevant postings. If in doubt, read the FAQ (Frequently Asked Questions) documents, which are regularly posted to most newsgroups. These documents will tell you all about the newsgroup, its functions, its rules, and answer many of the queries you may have. Whenever possible, check the FAQ before you submit a question to the newsgroup. If you cannot find any FAQs immediately, wait for a few days and one will almost undoubtedly be posted by one of the newsgroup regulars. Alternatively, you can post a request for the FAQ. If in doubt, 'lurk' for a while, reading the contributions from the regulars and old-timers, before diving in yourself.

Try to keep your postings well written, concentrate on being as concise as possible. Good spelling and grammar are important. You may not feel that these qualities should be important in what is basically a very informal medium, but it makes your posting much easier for other people to read and understand. Furthermore, people are more likely to read your posting than skip over it, or give up half way through. An eloquent piece is much more interesting to read, and much more persuasive.

Make sure that the line length setting of your text editor or word-processor program is not too long, and definitely not more than 80 characters, since most people read Network News using an 80 column display or window. Otherwise, your lines may wrap-around making your article very difficult and confusing for other people to read. You can always make your lines shorter by adding extra carriage-returns where appropriate (i.e. by pressing *return* or *enter*).

When writing a follow-up article, most news reader programs allow you to include portions of the original article as quotes. This may be useful if you wish to write separate responses to each point in the original article.

However, do not overdo it - it can be very tedious to read articles that consist mostly of quotes from earlier articles. Such articles are usually rather confusing to the reader, especially for anyone who has not followed the thread since its beginning. You should not post a follow-up article that is really only of interest to the person who posted the original article. Instead, you should e-mail your response to that person. It is also important to have your facts straight when posting articles. Much aggravation can be caused by posting inaccurate information.

Since the majority of newsgroup articles still tend to originate from North America, articles are commonly littered with acronyms and other abbreviations that you are expected to understand, such as IMHO (in my humble opinion), FAQ (frequently asked questions), FYI (for your information), BTW (by the way), CU (see you / bye), Objoke (obligatory joke follows), WRT (with respect to) and RTFM (read the *** manual)! For a new user, these may be a little puzzling. If you really must use these, try and stick to the well-known ones.

You may also come across what are called 'smilies' within messages, such as the basic :-) and the depressed :-(face. Look at these by turning the book 90 degrees clockwise. They are used within messages to indicate humour, sadness and other emotions. If you capitalise words LIKE THIS, it means that these words are shouted! Using asterisks like *this* is a way of emphasising particular words.

Network News is open to many millions of people, is largely unregulated and provides a certain degree of social anonymity to contributors, since you are very unlikely to ever meet most of them. When reading Network News, you will often come across what is called a 'flame', which is an unreasonably aggressive and even abusive response to an earlier message. Some threads seem to consist almost entirely of flame messages, particularly in some of the *alt* newsgroups. Some people enjoy posting deliberately provocative and controversial articles, in order to attract flame follow-ups, and hence these messages are called 'flame-bait'. Two or more people may get involved in exchanging 'flame' messages, in which case, we have what is called a 'flame war'. Sometimes these flames are clearly not very serious and may even be vaguely humorous, in a black or sarcastic way. However, at other times they can be quite 'close to the bone' and it is possible that people may be seriously offended. Many readers of Network News are amused by flames, whilst others think they are simply a manifestation of immaturity. In general, it is not recommended that flames be posted or responded to, since they are neither constructive nor intelligent, and only serve to waste resources on the network.

Chapter 7

EXPLORING THE INTERNET

There are now vast repositories of information and computer files stored on Internet computers all around the world. To unleash the full potential of the Internet, you need to be able to find and retrieve such data quickly and easily, wherever it might be located. To help you do this there are special computers called 'information servers' which will help to provide you with what you want, and programs which allow you to 'explore' Internet computers all over the planet, without moving from your keyboard. In this chapter we define what an information server is, and show you how they can help you. We also describe the four most important methods for exploring the Internet, which are called Archie, WAIS, Gopher and World Wide Web. With these tools, you will have the entire Internet and a world of information at your disposal.

What are Internet Information Servers?
An information server is a computer that provides users with a store of information, on any subject. It may also store other files, such as programs, pictures and graphics, audio, and other data. There are many such computers that are also Internet hosts and hence, can be accessed by members of the public via the Internet. Collectively, all these Internet information servers form a vast database distributed around the world.

A variety of methods, or protocols, have been developed to provide users of the Internet with access to the Internet information servers. In this chapter, four popular protocols are described, called Archie, WAIS (Wide Area Information Servers), Gopher and WWW (World Wide Web). They each have their own merits and drawbacks, as discussed below. All of these methods may be used, either by logging-in directly to the Internet information server with a program like Telnet, or by using a special 'client' program on a computer connected to the Internet, which provides a link between you and the server, and allows you to access the information on the server.

Archie

An Archie information server will search a selection of anonymous FTP sites for a file name or directory that you specify. When the search is completed, you will receive a list of the FTP sites and also the names of the directories at those sites, that contain the file you want.

There are three ways of getting information from Archie servers. Firstly, you can use an Archie client program, which resides on an Internet host computer, and will automatically connect you to an Archie server and set it working on your queries. Secondly, you can log-in directly to an Archie server with a user name of 'archie' and use that. Thirdly, you can send requests to Archie servers by e-mail.

To use an Archie client program, you must have an account on an Internet host computer that has an Archie client program. So, from your PC or Macintosh, you may have to log-in to this computer using a program such as Telnet. Once you have logged-in, type *archie filename* at the prompt and it will start searching for files with the name *filename*. This may take a few seconds, and the Archie server will normally tell you how long it expects to take. It will then display a list of all the Internet anonymous FTP sites that have relevant files, including the full IP host name of each computer, and the directory in which each file occurs. If there are a lot of results, you may want to enter the command *set pager*, before you start, so that the results will be displayed one page at a time. By default, Archie will ignore the case of the letters in *filename*. For example, *archie chess* might return files called *Chess* and *CHESS*. If you want to make Archie sensitive to case, use *archie -c filename* instead. If you are not sure of the exact file name, you may want to use *archie -s string*, which returns all files whose names include the letters in *string*. For example, *archie -s chess* might return files like *chess.zip, Zchess, chess.sit.hqx* , etc. You can even use a 'pattern', which Archie can use to pick files. Such a pattern is called a 'regular expression', and to use this search mode you would enter *archie -r regex*, where *regex* is the regular expression. The regular expression can contain special characters such as:

*	matches any number of whatever it follows
[xyz]	matches any one of the characters in the brackets
^	matches the beginning of the name
$	matches the end of the name; and a full-stop matches any one character.

For example *archie -r z*.zip* would return all files with *z* at the beginning and *.zip* at the end.

Alternatively, you may connect directly to an Archie information server using a program such as Telnet. There are quite a few to choose from, such as:

archie.doc.ic.ac.uk	UK
archie.au	Australia
archie.nz	New Zealand
archie.uqam.ca	Canada
archie.ans.net	USA
archie.luth.se	Sweden
archie.th-darmstadt.de	Germany
archie.rediris.es	Spain

When you have a connection, log-in with the user name 'archie'. No password is normally required. When you are connected, an Archie service will firstly display a welcome message on your screen, and will then present you with a prompt.

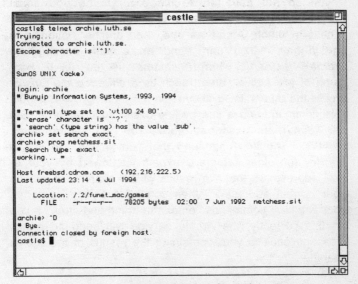

```
═══════════════════════════════ castle ══════════════════════════════
castle$ telnet archie.luth.se
Trying...
Connected to archie.luth.se.
Escape character is '^]'.


SunOS UNIX (acke)

login: archie
# Bunyip Information Systems, 1993, 1994

# Terminal type set to 'vt100 24 80'.
# `erase' character is '^?'.
# `search' (type string) has the value `sub'.
archie> set search exact
archie> prog netchess.sit
# Search type: exact.
working... =

Host freebsd.cdrom.com    (192.216.222.5)
Last updated 23:14  4 Jul 1994

    Location: /.2/funet_mac/games
      FILE   -r--r--r--    78205 bytes  02:00  7 Jun 1992  netchess.sit

archie> ^D
# Bye.
Connection closed by foreign host.
castle$ ▊
```

Figure 7.1 Using the Archie information server
on the site archie.luth.se.

From this point, you have similar Archie facilities to those described above, but the commands you should use are slightly different. At the prompt, type *prog string* and it will start searching for files whose names contain *string*. Remember that by default, Archie will ignore the case of the letters in *string*. For example, *prog chess* might return files called *Chess, CHESS, chess.zip, Zchess*, etc. If you want to make Archie sensitive to case, enter *set search subcase* before you start your search. To return to the default setting, which is not case sensitive, then enter *set search sub*. If you are sure of the exact file name, to speed up the search you should enter *set search exact* and then enter *prog filename*, where *filename* is the exact file name, including capitalisation. If you want to use a 'regular expression', as described above, then enter *set search regex* prior to your search.

If you do not have an Archie program on your local Internet host computer, and you cannot use Telnet to access a remote Archie service, then another option is to use e-mail. You can send an e-mail message to *archie@hostname*, where *hostname* is the full IP host name of the Archie server, such as *archie.doc.ic.ac.uk*, or any of the others listed above. In the message, you should give commands on a line by line basis, such as *prog* and *set search*, as described above for Archie information servers. The first command that you should use is *set mailto* (on older servers use *path*) followed by your e-mail address, so that the results of the search are sent to your correct address. When you have finished entering your retrieval commands, enter the command *quit.* If you do this correctly, the Archie service will send an e-mail message back to you, containing the results of the Archie search.

Once you have identified the exact name of the file you want, and its location, it should be a simple matter to retrieve it using FTP, as described in Chapter 4.

Wide Area Information Servers (WAIS)

Wide Area Information Servers (WAIS) are another way of finding files and information across the Internet. The WAIS concept was initially developed through collaboration by Thinking Machines, Apple Computers, and Dow Jones, and was introduced in 1991. WAIS was designed to provide a simple method for remote network users to access and retrieve information from a database stored on a central server computer, by looking for matches to a keyword supplied by the user. Unlike

Archie, which just looks at file names, WAIS also examines the contents of each file for matches with the keyword. There are now a number of WAIS databases, known as 'sources', that can be reached via the Internet or BBSs. WAIS can do quick keyword searches through a large number of such sources simultaneously.

One easy way of using WAIS is to remotely log-in to a Internet WAIS site, using a Telnet program. Well-known WAIS sites include the following:

Internet address	Country	Log-in user name
quake.think.com	USA	wais
swais.cwis.uci.edu	USA	swais
sunsite.unc.edu	USA	swais
info.funet.fi	Finland	wais

Simply Telnet to one of these sites and log-in with the user name 'wais' or 'swais' ('swais' stands for the Unix program Simple WAIS that these sites use). No password is necessary. After you have logged-in you may be asked to enter your e-mail address, and the type of terminal you are using. Normally, the terminal type will be 'vt100', as described in Chapter 4, in the section on Telnet.

Once you have done this, the WAIS program will display a list of available servers around the World, together with the sources they contain (although at the *quake.think.com* server, all the sources are under one heading). Although the cost of the source may be mentioned, do not worry. In practice they are all free. The important control keys are shown at the bottom of the WAIS display.

Firstly, decide which source you want to search. To move up and down the list of sources, press the arrow keys. To select a source, press the 'space bar'. An asterisk symbol shows that a source has been selected. If you want to de-select it later, highlight the item using the arrow keys and press the 'space bar' again. When you have selected the sources, you must enter the keywords you wish to search for. WAIS works best if a search is conducted using only a single keyword, otherwise you may get some unhelpful results. However, it is perfectly alright to try more than one keyword. To do this, press 'w', followed by the keywords, separated by spaces. Press *return* to start the search (Figure 7.2).

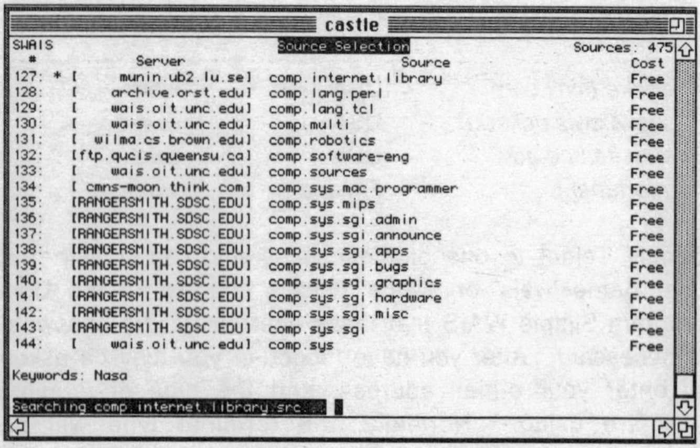

```
===============================  castle  ===============================
SWAIS                         Source Selection              Sources: 475
  #            Server                        Source                Cost
127: * [    munin.ub2.lu.se]  comp.internet.library          Free
128:   [    archive.orst.edu]  comp.lang.perl                 Free
129:   [    wais.oit.unc.edu]  comp.lang.tcl                  Free
130:   [    wais.oit.unc.edu]  comp.multi                     Free
131:   [  wilma.cs.brown.edu]  comp.robotics                  Free
132:   [ftp.qucis.queensu.ca]  comp.software-eng              Free
133:   [    wais.oit.unc.edu]  comp.sources                   Free
134:   [ cmns-moon.think.com]  comp.sys.mac.programmer        Free
135:   [RANGERSMITH.SDSC.EDU]  comp.sys.mips                  Free
136:   [RANGERSMITH.SDSC.EDU]  comp.sys.sgi.admin             Free
137:   [RANGERSMITH.SDSC.EDU]  comp.sys.sgi.announce          Free
138:   [RANGERSMITH.SDSC.EDU]  comp.sys.sgi.apps              Free
139:   [RANGERSMITH.SDSC.EDU]  comp.sys.sgi.bugs              Free
140:   [RANGERSMITH.SDSC.EDU]  comp.sys.sgi.graphics          Free
141:   [RANGERSMITH.SDSC.EDU]  comp.sys.sgi.hardware          Free
142:   [RANGERSMITH.SDSC.EDU]  comp.sys.sgi.misc              Free
143:   [RANGERSMITH.SDSC.EDU]  comp.sys.sgi                   Free
144:   [    wais.oit.unc.edu]  comp.sys                       Free

Keywords: Nasa

Searching comp.internet.library src...
```

Figure 7.2 WAIS keyword search in progress.

When the search is done, you are presented with a list of documents that contain the keywords. Each item has a score next to it that may range up to 1000: the higher the score, the greater the number of times your keyword was found (Figure 7.3). You can move the highlighted line up and down the list of documents using the arrow keys, and then select the one you want to read by pressing the 'space bar'. The document will be displayed on the screen, and if it is more than one page long, you can scroll through it by pressing the 'space bar'.

When you have finished reading a document, press 'q' to quit. You can then select another file to read. You can also save a selected file to the hard disk of the computer from which you are logged-in, by pressing 's'. Alternatively, you can get the WAIS server to mail you a copy of the file, by pressing 'l' (vertical bar) followed by *mail address,* where *address* is your normal e-mail address. To exit from WAIS, press 'q' once or twice, as necessary. There are several more commands besides those mentioned here. To get a full screen list of instructions on how to use WAIS, press '?'.

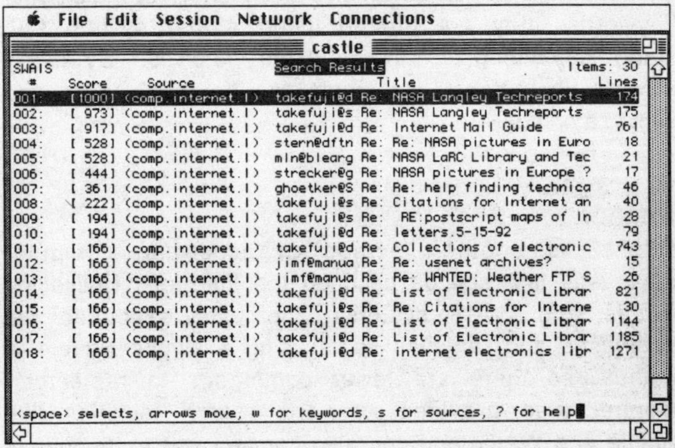

```
 File  Edit  Session  Network  Connections
                              castle
SWAIS                     Search Results              Items: 30
 #    Score   Source                    Title               Lines
001:  [1000] (comp.internet.I)  takefuji@d Re: NASA Langley Techreports  174
002:  [ 973] (comp.internet.I)  takefuji@s Re: NASA Langley Techreports  175
003:  [ 917] (comp.internet.I)  takefuji@d Re: Internet Mail Guide       761
004:  [ 528] (comp.internet.I)  stern@dftn Re: Re: NASA pictures in Euro  18
005:  [ 528] (comp.internet.I)  mln@blearg Re: NASA LaRC Library and Tec  21
006:  [ 444] (comp.internet.I)  strecker@g Re: NASA pictures in Europe ?  17
007:  [ 361] (comp.internet.I)  ghoetker@S Re: Re: help finding technica  46
008:  [ 222] (comp.internet.I)  takefuji@s Re: Citations for Internet an  40
009:  [ 194] (comp.internet.I)  takefuji@s Re:  RE:postscript maps of In  28
010:  [ 194] (comp.internet.I)  takefuji@d Re: letters.5-15-92           79
011:  [ 166] (comp.internet.I)  takefuji@d Re: Collections of electronic 743
012:  [ 166] (comp.internet.I)  jimf@manua Re: Re: usenet archives?       15
013:  [ 166] (comp.internet.I)  jimf@manua Re: Re: WANTED: Weather FTP S   26
014:  [ 166] (comp.internet.I)  takefuji@d Re: List of Electronic Librar 821
015:  [ 166] (comp.internet.I)  takefuji@s Re: Re: Citations for Interne   30
016:  [ 166] (comp.internet.I)  takefuji@d Re: List of Electronic Librar 1144
017:  [ 166] (comp.internet.I)  takefuji@s Re: List of Electronic Librar 1185
018:  [ 166] (comp.internet.I)  takefuji@d Re: internet electronics libr 1271

<space> selects, arrows move, w for keywords, s for sources, ? for help
```

Figure 7.3 Results of a WAIS search.

Instead of connecting directly to a WAIS site using Telnet, it is also possible to access WAIS sources by using a special client program on your PC or Macintosh, provided it is connected to the Internet. The freeware programs *Mosaic* and *Cello* both provide WAIS facilities to PC users. Another popular program for Microsoft *Windows* is *WinWais*. *PCWAIS* is a useful program for non-*Windows* users. There are comparable programs available for the Macintosh, such as *WAIStation* from

Apple Computers, *Mosaic*, and *WAIS for Mac*, all of which are freeware.

The *Windows* and Macintosh client programs provide user-friendly interfaces for WAIS, with pull-down menus and on-screen buttons. They also allow pictures to be grabbed from the WAIS server and displayed immediately on the screen. For example, *WinWais* permits you to carry out searches as described above, but in a more user-friendly, *Windows* environment. Source databases are selected from a window. Keywords are entered into a dialogue box. When documents are found that match your keywords, they are graded using a star system (1-4 stars), depending on how good the match is. By simply clicking on buttons, documents can be read, saved and sent to a printer.

Gopher

Gopher is another method of accessing computer databases that can be used on the Internet. Unlike the Archie and WAIS systems, the user examines the databases and retrieves items using a simple system of menus, so there are fewer commands to remember. Gopher also provides keyword search facilities like Archie and WAIS, and can also connect you to computers that do not support Gopher by using Telnet instead. It was originally designed to provide a campus-wide information system at the University of Minnesota Microcomputer, Workstation, Networks Center in 1991. It has quickly burgeoned and is now used extensively all over the world. There are currently a very large number of Internet computer databases that can be accessed using Gopher, called 'gopher servers'. There are a number of public access Gopher servers that you can connect to using Telnet, such as those listed below:

Internet Address	Country	Log-in user name
gopher.brad.ac.uk	UK	info
info.anu.edu.au	Australia	info
infoslug.ucsc.edu	USA	gopher
gopher.sunet.se	Sweden	gopher
gopher.uv.es	Spain	gopher
gopher.th-darmstadt.de	Germany	gopher

To access these, simply Telnet to the server, log-in with the appropriate user name, and you are immediately presented with a gopher menu (Figure 7.4). No passwords are required. Typically you can move the cursor up and down the menu by using the cursor arrow keys, and then select the menu item by pressing *enter* or *return*. Alternatively, you can select the menu item by entering its number. Selecting a menu option leads to other menus, and also to files that you can download. To go back to the previous menu, press 'u' for up.

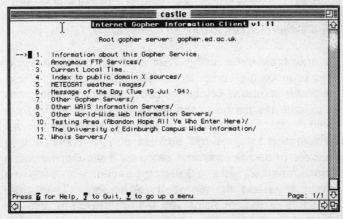

```
███████████████████████████ castle ███████████████████████████
              Internet Gopher Information Client v1.11

                 Root gopher server: gopher.ed.ac.uk

-->▌ 1.  Information about this Gopher Service.
    2.  Anonymous FTP Services/
    3.  Current Local Time.
    4.  Index to public domain X sources/
    5.  METEOSAT weather images/
    6.  Message of the Day (Tue 19 Jul '94).
    7.  Other Gopher Servers/
    8.  Other WAIS Information Servers/
    9.  Other World-Wide Web Information Servers/
   10.  Testing Area (Abandon Hope All Ye Who Enter Here)/
   11.  The University of Edinburgh Campus Wide Information/
   12.  Whois Servers/




Press ? for Help, Q to Quit, U to go up a menu            Page: 1/1
```

Figure 7.4 Gopher main menu.

As you move from menu to menu, you may wish to mark menus and menu items for later reference. To mark a menu, press 'A' (upper case), and to mark a menu item, press 'a' (lower case). To see a menu of all the marked items, press 'v' at any time. To delete an item from this menu, select it, and then press 'd'. These marks will only last until you quit and log-out.

Some Gopher menu items will automatically connect you to another computer database via Telnet. This enables you to access some powerful public database systems, such as libraries. You will be given a suggested user name and given the opportunity to log-in. The computer that you log-in to will provide you with instructions on what to do and how to use the system. When you have finished, log-out of the remote computer system, and you will be returned to the Gopher menu where you left off. Of course, you do not need to go through Gopher to use such a remote system. Once you have discovered a public database that you find useful, simply make a note of the IP host name and the user name for logging-in (and password too, if one is required). Then you can simply use a Telnet program to connect directly to it.

To download a file using Gopher, firstly use the arrow keys to move the cursor to the item that you want. Press the *enter* or *return* key to select the item, and then press 's' to save the file on to the computer from which you are using Telnet. Alternatively, if you press 'm', the file will be e-mailed to an e-mail address of your choice. It is possible to conduct keyword searches if the Gopher menu item is marked *<?>*. Select the menu item using the cursor keys and the *enter* or *return* key. Then enter keywords or the file name you wish to search for into the box that appears on the screen. Gopher will then produce a menu of items that match your request. Another way to conduct searches in Gopher, is by using a program called *veronica*. *Veronica*, usually spelled with a lower-case 'v', is an acronym for Very Easy Rodent-Orientated Net-wide Index to Computerized Archives, and was written at the University of Nevada. *Veronica* has more advanced search capabilities than the normal Gopher search and is usually an option that can be selected from the main Gopher menu. The *veronica* program will request you to enter a keyword, and will then search all the available Gopher menus for matches. You can then select those menu items. When you have finished using the Gopher server, press 'q' to exit.

Instead of connecting directly to a Gopher server by using Telnet, it is also possible to access Gopher servers by using a special Gopher client program on your PC or Macintosh, provided it is connected to the Internet. Good freeware PC programs for navigating around Gopher include *Mosaic, Cello, WinGopher* and *Hgopher*. There are Macintosh programs too, such as *TurboGopher, MacGopher*, and *GopherApp*.

The *Windows* and Macintosh Gopher client software packages provide a user-friendly interface for Gopher, with most options being available from pull-down menus and by pushing buttons on-screen. They may provide other extra facilities, such as allowing pictures to be downloaded from the Gopher source and displayed on the screen immediately. For example, *Hgopher* for *Windows* presents Gopher menu items within a window. Items can be selected by clicking on the adjacent icons. The spectacles icon means a text file, the 1101 icon means a binary file, the arrow icon means another menu and the terminal icon means a Telnet connection to another computer. *Hgopher* allows you to conduct searches, to mark items, and to download files.

A common feature of Gopher client programs is the ability to mark your favourite Gopher locations by placing what is called a 'bookmark'. Once you have placed a bookmark, you can return more quickly and easily to the specified location simply by selecting the bookmark. How you add a bookmark depends on which software you are using, but it should be found as a option within one of the menus. Note that your bookmarks may not always work if the network becomes busy, or some changes are made at the site of interest by the local system managers. In the latter case, you may have to set your bookmarks again.

World Wide Web (WWW)

World Wide Web, also known simply as 'WWW', 'W3' and 'the Web', is a relatively new method for accessing information servers. The rapidly growing popularity of WWW is partly due to the ease of use, and to the high quality way in which information may be presented, including high resolution colour graphics and pictures, as well as sound. Developed at CERN, the European Centre for Particle Physics, in 1991, the WWW system is different from both Gopher and WAIS in the way it accesses and presents information. It does not use a menu driven system like Gopher, nor is it based on a keyword search system like WAIS (although it can do this as well).

Instead, information is provided as pages of text, graphics, pictures, etc., one page at a time. Within each page of information, one or more 'link' words, pictures, or graphic icons are highlighted (or numbered). By selecting these links the user can move on to another page of related information, and from there to another page, and so on. These links may take you to pages on the same computer, or some other computer elsewhere in the world. Moving from page to page like this is called 'navigating'.

The method used by the WWW to store information is a version of the 'hypertext' database system, known as

HTML (Hypertext Mark-up Language). The WWW uses a communication protocol similar to HTTP (Hypertext Text Transfer Protocol), which is a public domain protocol compatible with TCP/IP (described in Chapter 3). WWW pages are referenced by URL (Universal Resource Locators), which give the precise location on the Internet. This consists firstly of the Internet site name, followed by the directory and any subdirectory names, and finally, the name of the file, all of which are separated by slashes ('/').

There are a number of WWW servers on the Internet that may be accessed by using Telnet, including those listed below:

www.njit.edu	USA
info.cern.ch	Switzerland
info.funet.fi	Finland
vms.huji.ac.il	Israel

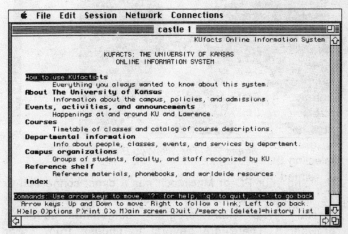

Figure 7.5 WWW server at the University of Kansas.

If you are asked for a user name when logging-in, use 'www'. Passwords are not required. Once you are connected to a WWW server, you are presented with a welcome page. Typically, the cursor can be moved to the desired link word using the *tab* key, or the arrow keys, and the link word is then selected by pressing *return* or *enter*. If the links are displayed as numbers inside brackets, then enter the relevant number. Important control keys are usually displayed at the bottom of each page of information. When you select a link, the relevant page is then displayed.

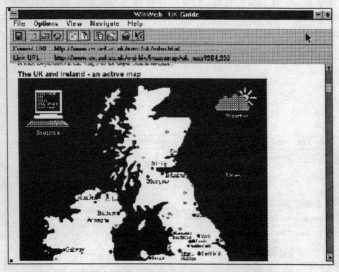

Figure 7.6 The WinWeb Browser.

Providing your PC or Macintosh has a direct connection to the Internet, another way of using WWW is to use a special WWW client program, sometimes called a 'browser'. There are several to choose from. For example, *WinWeb* is a well-known WWW browser (Figure 7.6) that runs in the *Windows* environment, and provides users with the ability to connect to any WWW server.

From there, users can wander from archive to archive around the world.

For *Windows* users, other similar WWW browsers include *Mosaic*, *Netscape*, and *Cello*. NCSA *Mosaic* is freeware and *Netscape* from Netscape Communications Corporation is currently free to non-business users (Figure 7.7). *Mosaic* and *Netscape* are also available for Macintoshes, and are popular ways of accessing the WWW.

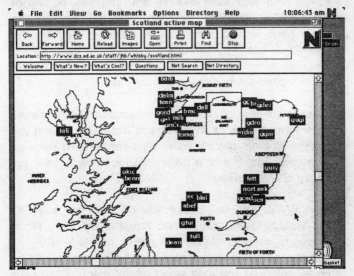

Figure 7.7 The Netscape browser for Macintosh.

The example above shows an active map from the Scottish Malt Whisky Tour. Each map label represents a distillery, and clicking on a label reveals several pages of information about the history and whisky at that distillery.

The *Windows* and Macintosh WWW browsers provide WWW functions via buttons and pull-down menus. Hypertext link words may be selected by moving the mouse and clicking the mouse button. When you select a link, your WWW browser downloads all the pages of text, graphics, pictures and audio associated with it. If there is a large amount of data to be downloaded, it may take several minutes. Your WWW browser should offer you the option to abort at any stage, should the download take too long. If you do not have a good quality colour monitor, you may also wish to select the text-only download option. Any of the text or other images that appear on your screen can be saved onto your hard disk as text, graphics, picture or sound files in standard formats. To go back to the previous page should simply be a matter of clicking the appropriate button. To go back to some other page should be possible also, by selecting it from pull-down menu of pages visited, sometimes called a 'history list'.

You can store the location of your favourite WWW pages using programs such as *WinWeb* and *Netscape*, so that you can return to them quickly later. You can set any page as your 'home page', i.e. the page that loads each time you start your WWW browser.

Certain WWW servers, called 'search engines', such as *ElNet Galaxy, Jumpstation* and *World Wide Web Worm* allow you to conduct keyword searches on the WWW. All pages that contain references to the keyword will be listed for you, and you may select any of them. Each page listed is scored to indicate how relevant the page may be, and also the size of the page. This provides a short-cut method of finding information about certain subjects, which is a useful alternative to the hypertext method.

WWW can also link you to Internet sites that do not yet support WWW, by using either Telnet, FTP or Gopher, whichever is most appropriate. This is done automatically for you, when you select certain hypertext links. When you exit from that site, you are returned to the WWW environment. This flexibility means that more and more services are becoming available to WWW users, such as access to Network News (described in Chapter 6), various public libraries, dictionaries (such as the *Oxford English Dictionary*), encyclopaedias (such as *Encyclopaedia Britannica*), newspapers (such as *The Guardian* and the *Daily Telegraph*), mail-order firms, and BBS services.

World Wide Web is rapidly becoming one of the most popular ways of interacting with the Internet. If you explore the WWW you will discover a large number of pages that are still being 'constructed'. Indeed, wandering through the WWW feels similar to wandering around a half-built city, because there is so much promise of further developments. The WWW may be superseded in the future by even more flexible, user friendly and powerful Internet programs, but at the time of writing, it represents the 'state of the art', and will probably be an important facet of the evolving 'information superhighway' for some time to come.

Appendix 1

GLOSSARY

Account Comprises the user name, password and home directory that each person should have, if they are registered on a multi-user computer or network.

Anonymous FTP Anonymous File Transfer Protocol. A standard method which allows a person at one computer to log-in to another computer as a guest and transfer files between the computers. Note that the person does not need to be registered on the remote computer, but the remote computer does need to be specially configured to accept anonymous FTP. FTP programs are abundant for PCs, Macintoshes and many other types of computer.

Apple Computers A US-based multinational company which makes the Macintosh, Quadra and Power Macintosh, and a whole host of printers, scanners, and other peripherals. Apple Computers were amongst the first to popularise the use of WIMP (windows, icon, mouse and pointer) as a method of controlling desktop computers. Apple Computers do not make PCs, which have for many years rivalled Apple's range of computers.

Application is another term for a computer program, or suite of programs.

Archie A program found on many Internet host computers, which allows the user to conduct searches for particular files across the Internet. Archie will list file and directory locations comprising host computer names and directory paths.

Arcnet A network system developed by Standard Microsystems Corporation for use with PCs.

ARPANET Advanced Research Projects Agency Network. The forerunner of the modern Internet which was established in 1969 for the United States military, and eventually dismantled in 1990.

ASCII American Standard Code for Information Interchange. ASCII code provides a way of representing binary numbers as ordinary alphabetic, numeric, and keyboard characters, using 128 ASCII characters. An ASCII character file is a very common, simple way of storing text in a computer or on a disk. ASCII can also be used to code and store any kind of binary file.

ATM Asynchronous Transfer Mode. A new protocol for sending information around global networks. The information sent is electronically pre-packaged and addressed before sending, using a standard format. There is no need for the receiving computer to be synchronised with the sending computer, before information is sent.

Attachment This a file that is sent with an e-mail message. Synonymous with 'enclosure'.

BABT British Approvals Board for Telecommunications. Only modems approved by the BABT can be used legally in the UK. A green BABT Approved circle means that your modem is approved. A red triangle means that it is not approved.

Backbone A large, high-capacity and fast network system which connects a variety of smaller networks, e.g. NSFNET, which connects large computers and LANs within the USA.

Back-up A copy of a file, a directory, or a hard disk, or a secondary electronic device, which means that there are fewer problems if the original is destroyed, corrupted or lost by accident.

Bandwidth This is a general term for the rate at which data is sent through a network. A high bandwidth means that large amounts of data can be sent quickly. Network users who send unnecessarily large files down the network are often accused of taking up too much bandwidth, because sending large files can slow down the network for other users.

Baud In a binary system, the Baud rate is the number of bits transmitted per second. This is one way of measuring the speed at which computer data is transmitted. This measure is now used much less frequently than the alternative BPS (Bits Per Second).

BBS Bulletin Board System. Originally this meant a computer network that provided users with the ability to contribute news and messages, and allowed all other users to read these contributions, and if they wished, respond to them. Most BBSs are now commercial, and provide users with many other services, such as Internet access, electronic mail, news and weather information, etc.

Binary A counting system that uses ones and zeros only, rather than the numbers zero through to nine. All computers function at their most basic level by using binary, since they run on electricity, and electricity can be used to code one (on) and zero (off). Many computer files store data as binary numbers.

BinHex A method for coding any computer file using ASCII characters only (i.e. text). Also the name of a program that can code and decode BinHex files.

Bit Binary digit, i.e. one or zero. Bits are a useful way of expressing the two main electrical states, respectively on and off. Any number that can be expressed using the binary counting system can be represented using a series of bits.

Bit-map A method for storing pictures or letters on a screen or in a file using binary code.

BITNET Because It's There Network, or alternatively, Because It's Time Network. A co-operative network for academic institutions established in the USA, but now used around the world. It is more primitive than the Internet, being best for electronic mail and file transfer only, rather than interactive services such as Telnet.

BPS Bits Per Second. This specifies the speed of data transfer, defined by the number of bits (binary digits) transferred per second. The term is often used to describe the speed at which networks and modems work.

Bridge A device that can connect different and even incompatible LANs, whether they are on the same site or in different locations, when the remote link is provided by a WAN. Also, see 'gateway'.

Browser A program used to explore the World Wide Web.

Bulletin board See BBS.

Byte A number consisting of 8 binary digits or 'bits'. In the decimal counting system, a byte can have values of 0-255. Data on a computer or hard disk is commonly stored as bytes, since a byte can represent one of up to 256 alphabetic, numeric and other characters.

Case sensitive Sometimes it does not make any difference whether you use upper case (capital) letters or lower case letters when entering text into a computer. If it is important that you use the correct case, then the computer or program is said to be 'case sensitive'.

CD-ROM Compact Disk-Read Only Memory. A disk upon which digital data has been pre-recorded, which can be read using a CD-ROM 'drive' connected to a computer. CD-ROM data is stored using optical techniques rather than the magnetic techniques that are used for conventional floppy disks, and hence data can not be erased with magnetic fields. In fact, data on a CD-ROM may not be changed in any way. The technology is the same as that used for ordinary music CDs, hence CD-ROM drives can be used to play music CDs, providing your computer has a sound card, loudspeakers or headphone jack and the appropriate software.

CIX Compulink Information Exchange. A network based on the TCP/IP standard, which permits commercial usage, unlike the Internet.

Client computer A computer which relies upon the resources of another, usually more powerful computer, to which it is connected. In a typical server-based network, all the computers connected to the server computer may be called clients.

Client program A program that relies upon the resources of another program, usually residing on another computer, to which there is a network connection. For example, PC and Macintosh 'Gopher' and 'World Wide Web' programs are client programs which are used to access Internet information server computers.

Clipboard Users of *Windows* and Macintoshes always have a temporary file available for storing text and graphics, which is called the 'clipboard'. When you 'copy' or 'cut' text or graphics in a word processing package, graphics program, or any other application, the text or graphics is stored in the clipboard file. You can view what is in this file at any time by selecting the clipboard icon. When you use any application's 'paste' function, the contents of the clipboard are added to the file that you are working on with that application.

CompuServe One of the largest multinational Bulletin Board Systems and providers of Internet services to business and non-business clients.

Conference Part of a Bulletin Board System which is set aside for discussion and messaging on a chosen subject.

COSE Common Open Software Environment. Under this 1993 agreement, all major Unix developers consented to adhere to a set standard for Unix application interfaces, providing software for incompatible Unix applications to operate across different platforms.

CPU Central Processing Unit. This is the silicon chip at the heart of every computer which performs all the logical operations, including calculations, under the direction of programs stored in the memory. CPUs are manufactured by a variety of manufacturers, and many different designs are available, with differing performance characteristics.

CSNET Computer Science Network. Founded in the early 1980's for universities, it became defunct in 1991.

Cyberspace A buzz-word of the mid-1990's, meant to describe the world of human interaction which is taking place wholly via electronic means on the Internet.

Data Any type of information that may be stored or processed by a computer. Data is stored in files, usually in either ASCII or binary format.

Database A collection of information or data, which is arranged in an orderly manner and stored in some kind of system which allows the data to be retrieved. There are large computer databases all over the world, many of which can be reached via the Internet.

Device Any piece of hardware other than a computer, such as a printer, a plotter, a scanner or a CD-ROM.

Dialogue box An on-screen box found in Macintosh windows or Microsoft *Windows*, in which you can make choices about what you want the computer to do next.

Directory This is a collection of files which have all been stored under a common name, on a hard disk or diskette. There are various ways of referring to a directory. In DOS, Unix, and VMS, directories have long names, depending on which disk drive they are on, and if they are themselves contained within another directory. In windows operating systems, such as that used on Macintoshes and Microsoft *Windows*, the directories are represented by icons. These icons often look like folders, and are referred to as such.

Disk drive An electronic device which will read and write magnetically coded data to and from a diskette or a hard disk. All PCs and Macintoshes have at least two disk drives, one for diskettes and one for the hard disk inside the computer.

Diskette See 'floppy disk'.

DNS Domain Name System. A hierarchical system for naming computers connected to the Internet, based on their country, their institutional affiliation, and local computer name. The DNS is used for IP host names.

Domain Part of an IP host name.

DOS Disk Operating System. This is a simple computer language which allows the user to control computer disk drives and other basic functions. IBM, Microsoft, and Novell all produce DOS programs for PCs. The PC is controlled by typing simple text commands. Microsoft *Windows 95* is more complex, since it is a DOS system and a windows system combined. Similarly, *System 7* from Apple Computers allows full control of a Macintosh and its disk system using icons and windows. Note that when most people refer to DOS, they are referring to DOS on a PC, but strictly speaking, every computer has a DOS installed.

Download This is the process of moving or copying a file (i.e. data or program) from a larger computer onto a smaller computer. When you are connected to a large network, or bulletin board, you will commonly be downloading files onto your PC or Macintosh.

Driver A program which allows a computer to interact with a hardware device such as a printer or a scanner. Different hardware from different manufacturers require different drivers to be installed on the computer.

Dumb terminal A screen and keyboard that uses the resources of another computer, but which is not a computer in its own right.

EMACS A text editor program commonly used on Unix computers. Another version is called 'MicroEMACS'.

E-mail Electronic mail. A message or computer file with a standard header, which is sent from one networked user to another. The other user may be on your LAN, or may be on the other side of the world.

Enclosure   This a file that is sent with an e-mail message. Synonymous with 'attachment'.

Encryption   A method for making a password secret. The password is coded in such a way that it cannot easily be read.

EPS   Encapsulated *PostScript*   A version of the *PostScript* language / code, which is used to send graphics and text to printers.

Ethernet   An international standard LAN technology, comprising specialised cables, adapter cards and associated software. This is probably the most popular and widespread LAN technology. Originally developed by Xerox, Ethernet was later standardised by Xerox, Digital Equipment and Intel. This is known as IEEE (Institute of Electrical and Electronics Engineers) standard 802.3. Three types of Ethernet now exist: Thin, Thick and Twisted-Pair.

EtherTalk   A communication protocol designed by the Apple Computer company that allows Macintosh computers to use an Ethernet network.

FAQ   Frequently Asked Questions. This is a file of information, commonly posted to Network News groups, which attempts to answer network users' most commonly asked questions. If you join a new newsgroup, try to read the FAQ, before asking the other readers too many questions about the newsgroup.

File   This is a block of data (text or other information), or a program, which is a discrete entity and has its own name. A file can be recorded on a hard disk drive or a diskette, sent to a peripheral device such as printer, or sent across a network.

File extension Refers to the part of a file name after the full-stop, e.g. *readme.txt* has the file extension *txt*. The file extension is usually only three letters and indicates the type of file and/or how it was produced, e.g. *txt* indicates that the file contains text. File extensions will be familiar to PC users but are rarely used for Macintosh files, since Macintosh files nearly always have an associated icon, which provides a visual description of the file type and usually also the program which produced it.

Flame A colloquial term used in Network News groups, which refers to a highly vitriolic response to a posting. Some Network News contributors enjoy making deliberately provocative and contentious postings, in order to attract flame responses. This is called 'flame bait'.

Floppy disk Also known as a diskette. This is a circular piece of magnetic material, which is indeed floppy, but is housed inside a rigid protective covering. Two main sizes exist. Diskettes that are 3.5 inches across are now most common, and are protected by a plastic shell. 5.25 inch diskettes are still sold, and these are protected by a much thinner shell. Most computers have a disk drive device that will record and retrieve programs and data from diskettes.

Freeware Software that is available for anyone to use, and does not need to be paid for. There is a plentiful supply of freeware available over the Internet. Not to be confused with shareware.

FTP File Transfer Protocol. A standard method which allows a person at one computer to log-in to another computer and transfer files between the computers. Programs that utilise FTP are abundant for PCs, Macintoshes and many other types of computer.

Gateway A computer link which allows two or more networks to communicate. All information and data which is sent from one network to another must go via the gateway. E-mail gateways are one example, allowing e-mail to be sent from one type of network to another.

Gb Gigabyte. One thousand million bytes. One byte is the equivalent of one alphabetic or numeric character. This term is generally used to define the size of computer memories and disks.

GIF Graphics Interchange Format. A binary data format for storing pictures.

Gigabyte See 'Gb'

Gopher A method for browsing the Internet and information stored in various large computers around the World. Users control Gopher via menus and simple commands. Files can also be downloaded using Gopher.

GUI Graphical User Interface. This is a way of controlling your computer by activating pictures (icons) which represent applications and files. Macintosh *System 7* is a GUI, and so is Microsoft *Windows*.

Hard disk Also referred to as 'hard disk drive' or 'hard drive'. This comprises a stack of magnetically coated aluminium disks fixed onto a spindle, which is housed inside your computer, and upon which programs and data can be stored. External hard disks sit outside the main computer housing, in a separate case.

Hardware This means the actual computer, printer, disk drive, etc., comprising silicon chips, plastic and metal! It specifically does not include the actual programs which are used to run the above devices and called software.

Header Information given at the top of a document or file, usually detailing what the document or file is about. For example, a word-processor text document may have a header that is printed at the top of each page and gives the title of the document. A computer file normally has a header that describes the file type, how the code is set out, how large the file is, etc. An e-mail message also has a header that describes who it is from, who it is to, when it was sent, etc.

Home directory The part of a hard disk on a LAN server computer or multi-user computer where users keep their personal files.

Host computer A computer on a network which allows remote users to use its facilities, i.e. it acts as a host. For example, most Internet computers are host computers. See 'IP host name' and 'IP host number'.

HTML Hypertext Mark-up Language. A version of the hypertext language used by the World Wide Web to create pages of text and pictures that are linked by highlighted words.

HTTP Hypertext Text Transfer Protocol. A public domain protocol compatible with TCP/IP, particularly useful for linking text databases on networked computers. Although it does not completely comply with the HTTP standard, the World Wide Web uses an HTTP-like system.

Hypertext A method for linking pages of text and pictures within a computer database or network service by using highlighted 'link' words. By selecting link words, the user can move easily from reading one topic to another.

IBM International Business Machines. A US-based multinational company which produced the original PC (Personal Computer), and is still producing its successors. However, many PCs are now made by companies other than IBM. IBM also produce a number of larger computers.

Icon A small picture which appears on a computer screen to represent a file, a program or some process that is taking place. It is used in conjunction with windows and a mouse to control the computer. Icons can be selected, moved, activated, and thrown away.

Information Superhighway A buzzword of the mid-1990's, meant to describe the evolving interconnected electronic networks which are linking homes, offices, schools and universities around the World. The Internet represents the first crude incarnation of the Information Superhighway. Ultimately the Information Superhighway will develop into a very sophisticated, all-embracing world-wide network.

Internet A computer communications network started in the US in the 1970's, which has since grown to encompass more than 20 million users world wide. It now comprises a loosely connected collection of networks, which communicate using simple standard protocols. Internet software and hardware is sold by a variety of vendors in different countries. Although there is locally some regulation of the Internet, there is no international control or ownership of the Internet.

IP Internet Protocol. These are the rules and standards of the Internet, which allow such a huge variety of computers and software packages to interact with the Internet, and with each other via the Internet.

IP host name Every computer connected to the Internet must have an identifying name, which is called the IP host name. The form is usually three to five alphabetic codes, separated by full-stops. These codes indicate the actual name of the computer or LAN, the organisation and type of organisation (academic, commercial, government or military), and the country.

IP host number Every computer connected to the Internet must have an identifying code number, which is called the IP number. The form of the IP host number is usually four numbers separated by full-stops.

ISDN Integrated Services Digital Network. High-speed private communications link, which is paid for only when used.

IT Information Technology. This is another term for the general field of computer communications and data/information retrieval.

JANET Joint Academic NETwork. An incarnation of the Internet which exists in the UK only. It was created jointly by British academic institutions.

JPEG A binary data format for storing pictures devised by the Joint Photographic Experts Group.

Kb Kilobyte. One thousand bytes. One byte is the equivalent of one alphabetic or numeric character. This term is generally used to define the size of computer memories and disks.

Kermit An error-correcting file transfer protocol designed for connecting computers to a network with a dial-up link. It was developed at Columbia University in the early 1980's. It has been adapted for use with Ethernet networks.

Kilobyte See Kb

LAN Local Area Network. A group of computers which communicate with each other via special electrical cables, hardware and software. A LAN may also include printers, communal disk drives, and other peripherals. Typically, a LAN will encompass all the computers in one office, or in a few buildings at most.

LocalTalk A communication protocol developed for Macintosh LANs by the Apple Computer company.

Log-in The process of entering a user name and password when beginning a session on a multi-user computer or network. Also known as 'log-on'.

Log-out The process of finishing a session on a multi-user computer or network. Also known as 'log-off'.

Machine A word commonly used instead of 'computer'.

Macintosh This name covers a whole family of computers produced by the Apple Computer company. Its functions and performance are broadly similar to PCs, although it has a different operating system and runs different software. The Macintosh uses a 'windows' based operating system, the current version of which is called *System 7*, but this is not to be confused with the Microsoft *Windows* program for PCs.

Mailbox This is the location on a networked computer, that receives and stores a particular user's incoming e-mail messages. The mailbox always has a name, which is very often the same as the person's user name.

Mail folder A directory or folder on a disk that is used to store e-mail messages.

Mail program A computer program that handles e-mail.

Mainframe A very large and expensive multi-user computer, usually found only in large organisations that require powerful computing facilities.

Mb Megabyte. One million bytes. One byte is the equivalent of one alphabetic or numeric character. This term is generally used to define the size of computer memories and disks.

Megabyte See Mb.

Memory The silicon chips inside a computer that store data. See 'RAM' and 'ROM'.

MIME Multipurpose Internet Mail Extensions. A method for encoding files, particularly useful for sending images, audio and video files by e-mail.

Modem An abbreviation for modulator/demodulator. This is a hardware device which may be installed inside your computer, or as a free-standing unit outside your computer. You must also have the appropriate software to run the modem, although this is usually supplied with the modem. It allows you to connect your computer directly to a telephone line and thus enables you to send and receive data over the telephone.

Mouse The small gadget which sits beside most Macintoshes and PCs, with a lead connecting it to the computer, and one or more buttons on top. By sliding the mouse across the desk, preferably on a special mouse pad, and by pressing the mouse buttons, it is possible to control the computer, providing the computer is running software which recognises the mouse, as in all Macintoshes, and PCs running Microsoft *Windows*.

Net As in 'The Net', meaning the Internet.

Network A collection of computers and other devices such as printers and disk drives which are connected, such that they can communicate and send data from one to another.

Network News The world wide bulletin board system which is free to use, and is also known as 'Usenet' and 'net news'.

Newsfeed A computer that provides users with the ability to read Network News.

Newsgroup A forum for discussion within 'Network News', which has a common theme.

NSFNET National Science Foundation Network. This network was started in the United States in 1986, and links major computing centres around the country.

OLR Off-Line Reader. A program used to access data on a bulletin board. The program lets you do most of your work before and after accessing the bulletin board, saving telephone and access charges. You must firstly give it instructions about the data you want to access, so that when it logs on it will be able to perform the operation automatically and log-out quickly.

Operating system A program which controls the basic functions of a computer, such as the monitor screen, the keyboard and the disk drives.

OSI Open Systems Interconnection. A very complex computer communication protocol developed by a consortium of European standards organisations, the foremost of which is the ISO (International Standards

Organisation). Compared to TCP/IP, it is theoretically more flexible, but in practice it is unwieldy and difficult to implement.

Outernet All networks that are not part of the Internet.

Parallel port This is a socket at the back of a computer that receives or transmits data a byte at a time. It is sometimes called the 'printer port', since the socket can be used for connecting a printer. Compare with 'serial port'.

Password This is the secret code that a person on a multi-user computer network must enter when starting a session, i.e. logging-in. A password usually comprises about six alphanumeric characters.

Path This is a description of the route to a particular file, which may start with the name of the disk drive, followed by the name of a directory, followed by the names of any number of subdirectories, followed by the name of the file itself. For example, a typical DOS path might look like C:\text\letters\john.doc, where the disk drive is C, the directory is called 'text', the subdirectory is called 'letters' and the file is called john.doc.

PC Personal Computer. Originally produced by IBM, this computer has since been copied by many other manufacturers. Today's PC is a much more powerful machine than its predecessors. The name 'PC' is commonly given to any generic desktop or portable computer, which is compatible with IBM's standards. PCs commonly use DOS and/or Microsoft *Windows* as an operating system.

Peer-to-peer This is a small local area network, in which no computer is dedicated to acting as a server. All the machines on the network can act as both an ordinary networked machine, i.e. a client, and as a server.

Peripheral Generally a printer, plotter, scanner, CD-ROM or any other specialised piece of electronic hardware connected to a computer or network that provides a facility.

Pict A binary data format for storing pictures, mostly used by Macintoshes.

Platform Jargon for 'computer'. Hence, 'cross-platform integration' means making different types of computers work coherently together.

POP Post Office Protocol. A network standard for transmission of e-mail messages, which transfers messages from a mail server computer to a user's own computer.

Port This is the physical connection between your computer and any network or peripheral. If you look at the back of your computer, you should see at least one or two ports, which are in fact specialised sockets into which you can plug your network or peripheral cable. There are several types of ports, including serial, parallel and scsi.

Posting A contribution to one of the network news groups.

Postmaster A network system manager who is responsible for e-mail facilities on his or her network.

PostScript A language / code used to send text and graphics to printers and plotters.

Power PC / Power Macintosh Neither an ordinary Macintosh nor a PC, this machine will run both Macintosh and PC software. It is the result of collaboration between IBM and Apple Computers, who produce PCs and Macintoshes respectively. Although it is a relatively fast machine, it must do a lot of translation work to use such a variety of software, and this results in reduced performance. New software is now appearing which is specifically written for the Power PC / Power Macintosh, and this runs much faster.

PPP Point-to-Point Protocol. A protocol which enables the TCP/IP standard to be used over a serial link, such as a telephone line. Useful for modem users. Similar to SL/IP.

Privileges These are the individual 'rights' of a user on a multi-user computer or network, such as which files they may use, and which they may not, which printers they may use, and which they may not, etc.

Processor A silicon chip inside a computer that is designed to take incoming data and process it in some way. See CPU.

Protocol A protocol is any set of rules and standards that define how a computer or a network should work. Many simple computer network languages are referred to as protocols.

PSTN Public Switched Telephone Network. Telephone lines used for transmitting computer data.

RAM Random Access Memory. These are the silicon chips inside a computer that are used to store transient data. RAM only works whilst the power is on, so data needs to be saved onto a hard disk or other storage device, before the power is switched off. The amount of

RAM a computer has is one measure of how 'powerful' it is. Compare with 'ROM'.

Remote computer Any computer you can access other than the one you are sitting in front of. 'Remote' may refer to the other side of the room you are in, or the other side of the world.

RFC Request For Comments. RFCs are documents that detail Internet protocols, and how the Internet is run. New RFCs are written by those who wish to make changes to the Internet, or to clarify certain aspects, and these may or may not be accepted by the various volunteer committees and work groups who help to manage the Internet.

ROM Read Only Memory. These are silicon chips inside a computer that are used to store data permanently. Data in ROM is not lost when the power is switched off. Data in ROM can not be changed in any way. ROM is often used to store a very basic operating system for a computer, which immediately activates when the computer is switched on, so that the computer is then able to load the main operating system, such as *System 7* for a Macintosh or DOS for a PC. Compare with 'RAM' and 'CD-ROM'.

Router A computer within a network that controls the movement and forwarding of data and information 'packets'. The Internet has very many routers, that help to keep the electronic traffic moving.

Scanner A electronic device which can scan a paper document and convert the image into binary code. With the right software, a scanner is a useful way of getting text and pictures into a computer system.

Scsi Small computer systems interface. Pronounced 'scuzzy', this is a common means of connecting peripheral devices to your computer, such as printers, disk drives, etc. Most computers have at least one scsi port (or socket) on the back of the machine. In theory, scsi is standardised so that you can connect different devices from different manufacturers with equal ease. In practice, not all scsi devices connect well with all scsi computer ports.

Seamless This describes a network, or suite of software packages, where the links have been cleverly disguised or hidden, so that the user is either wholly or partially unaware that there are any links at all. Thus the software or network appears much simpler and easier for the user, whilst remaining fully functional.

Serial port This is a socket at the back of a computer that receives or transmits data a bit at a time. The serial port is also sometimes known as RS232. This socket on the back of a computer allows connection of an external modem, serial mouse and other peripherals. Compare with 'parallel port'.

Server Within a LAN, it is common for one machine to be dedicated as a server. It does just that - serves the other computers on the network, handling routine network management, such as running printers and scanners. The server is also likely to have some large disks, which may be shared by other machines on the network. The server will be left running unattended most of the time, except when the system manager has to fix things.

Shareware Software which you can try before you buy it. Shareware is commonly available over the Internet. If you continue to use the software, you should register with the producers and usually pay a small fee.

SL/IP Serial Line / Internet Protocol. A protocol which enables the TCP/IP standard to be used over a serial link, such as a telephone line. Useful for modem users who wish to make a direct link to the Internet. Similar to PPP.

SMTP Simple Mail Transfer Protocol. A standard for transmission of e-mail messages, and is particularly used within the Internet. This is the most common protocol used by Macintosh and PC networks.

Snail mail A facetious term for regular mail sent via the post office. Used by e-mail addicts, it of course refers to the fact that regular mail is so much slower than e-mail.

Software This is the programming code that resides inside the chips of your computer, and is recorded on your hard disk, and which you can buy on diskettes. The software is what makes your hardware do something useful!

Spool Simultaneous peripheral operation on-line. This is the process whereby a file to be printed is dumped onto a disk or tape drive, so that the computer can get on with other operations. When you send a document to be printed on a network, it is common for it to be spooled to a hard disk drive attached to the server. The document can then be passed to the printer when the printer is ready, and you can carry on using your computer whilst you wait for the document to be printed. This is all handled by special 'print spooler' software.

Stand alone computer A computer that has no network connections.

TCP/IP Transmission Control Protocol / Internet Protocol. This is a very widely used and fundamental collection of communication protocols utilised by the

Internet, and many networked PCs and Macintoshes. It is also used by a wide variety of other computer types.

Telnet A simple, but common protocol for accessing another computer remotely from your own, whether it be on the LAN or the Internet. Software which uses Telnet exists for most types of computer, such as the popular NCSA *Telnet* program. It effectively turns your computer into a terminal for the remote computer.

Terminal A terminal is a machine that allows a person to use the resources of a remote computer, and must comprise at least a monitor and keyboard, as well as the necessary connections to the remote computer. There are terminals that comprise a monitor and keyboard only, but are not computers in their own right - see 'Dumb terminal'. There are also programs which will turn a PC or Macintosh into a terminal, such as Telnet programs. See also 'VT100'.

Text editor A program that allows a user to compose and edit a file of text. Word-processor programs are really just very sophisticated text editors.

The Net Abbreviation for the Internet.

tn3270 A version of the Telnet protocol specifically tailored for use with the IBM standard terminal, the tn3270.

Token Ring An international standard LAN adapter promoted by IBM for PCs. Faster, but more expensive and less popular than Ethernet.

Transparent See 'seamless'.

Unix The most common operating system language on workstations such as those from Sun Microsystems and

Silicon Graphics. It is also found on larger computers, but generally is not used on PCs and Macintoshes. You may well come across it if you log-in to a larger computer from your PC or Macintosh. Originally developed by AT&T, Unix has been around for many years and versions have been marketed by IBM, Unisys, SCO, Digital Equipment and Hewlett-Packard, amongst others.

Upload This is the process of moving or copying a file (i.e. data or program) from a smaller computer onto a larger computer. When you are connected to a large network, or bulletin board, you may be able to upload files from your PC or Macintosh.

URL Uniform (or Universal) Resource Locators. A standard way of describing the location of a file on the Internet: first the name of site, then the directory, and then the name of the file, all separated by slashes ('/').

Usenet An abbreviation for 'Users' Network'. A global network service for academic and commercial organisations which was started in the late 1970's. Its main role now is to provide a conferencing system, better known as Network News.

User name The unique identity code for each person who is registered on a multi-user computer or network. A user name usually comprises alphanumeric characters that bear some relation to the user's real name.

UUCP A world wide network developed for users of Unix computers, but now serving other users including PC and Macintosh users. The acronym originally stands for Unix-to-Unix Copy Program.

Uuencode Unix to Unix encode. A method for coding any file using ASCII characters only (i.e. text). Particularly used within Network News.

UUNET A non-profit network designed to provide access to USENET Network News, various computer archives, and e-mail facilities.

Vax A type of mainframe computer produced by the Digital Equipment Corporation.

Veronica Very Easy Rodent-Orientated Net-wide Index to Computerized Archives (normally spelled with a lower-case 'v'). A program written at the University of Nevada which permits keyword searches to be done on Gopher information servers.

Vi A text editor program commonly used on Unix computers.

VMS A computer operating system developed for Vax mainframe computers. It is now less popular than the rival Unix operating system. It is generally not used on PCs and Macintoshes, but you may well come across it if you log-in to a larger computer from your PC or Macintosh. IBM DOS was originally developed from VMS, so that now, IBM DOS, Microsoft DOS and Novell DOS all have many commands in common with VMS, such as DIR, CD, DEL, and many others.

VT100 Historically, this was originally a widely used type of computer terminal manufactured by the Digital Equipment Corporation. It was a primitive monochrome text-only display. The format of the VT100 screen has since become a kind of standard display type. Many different kinds of computers can emulate the VT100, including PCs and Macintoshes, provided they have the right software.   This is important for increased compatibility. It is particularly used for Telnet sessions.

WAIS Wide Area Information Servers. A way of locating and extracting files from large databases, such as those found on the Internet. WAIS searches for files using keywords which the user enters.

WAN Wide Area Network. A computer network that may be national or global in extent, and which may use a variety of communication links, such as dedicated electrical or optical cables, telephone lines, radio or satellite links. Most WANs are used in the commercial environment.

White pages directory A computer database containing people's e-mail addresses, and possibly also postal addresses, telephone numbers, etc. If the database is on the Internet it is usually easily accessible via Gopher or World Wide Web.

WIMP Acronym standing for windows, icon, mouse and pointer.

Windows A window is a rectangular area, usually with some graphical scrolling devices at the sides, and a menu at the top, which allows you to manipulate your computer or run a program. Most computers allow the user to use the computer via several windows which may be displayed on the screen at the same time, often overlapping one another. Macintoshes have always used windows, via a system developed by Apple Computers. Window systems have now become very popular on the PC also, especially Microsoft *Windows*, which is what is often meant by people using the term 'windows'.

WWW World Wide Web. This is a protocol for accessing computers and databases world wide over the Internet. Developed at CERN, the European Centre for Particle Physics, in 1991. It uses the hypertext system for accessing text and picture databases.

X.25 A communications protocol designed for larger networks and WANs, and for large commercial users. It is designed to receive data in packets, the arrival times of which are uncertain. This is particularly suited to data transmission, but not interactive use of software over the network.

X.500 Developed by the CCITT (Comite Consultatif International Telegraphique et Telephonique), this is a network protocol specifically designed to handle large databases that are distributed across a network of computers. It is widely used for large address, telephone and e-mail directories. X.500 was designed to be compatible with the OSI communications protocol.

Appendix 2

BULLETIN BOARD SYSTEM AND INTERNET VENDOR ADDRESSES

Auntie
BBC Networking Club
Room S401, Sulgrave House
London, W12 8QT

CityScape Internet Services Ltd.
Alexandria House
Covent Garden
Cambridge, CB1 3JE

Compulink Information Exchange (CIX)
Suite 2, The Sanctuary
Oakhill Grove
Surbiton
Surrey, KT6 6DU

CompuServe
1 Redcliff Street
P.O. Box 676
Bristol, BS99 1YN

Connect BBS
P.O. Box 360
Harrow, HA1 4LQ

Demon Internet Ltd.
Gateway House
322 Regents Park Road
Finchley
London, N3 2QQ

EUnet GB
Wilson House
John Wilson Business Park
Whitstable
Kent, CT5 3QY

eWorld
Apple Computer UK Ltd.
6 Roundwood Avenue
Stockley Park
Uxbridge
Middlesex, UB11 1BB

Frontier Internet Service Ltd.
1st Floor
45 Hatton Garden
London, EC1N 8EX

Microsoft Ltd.
Microsoft Place
Winnersh
Wokingham
Berkshire, RG11 5TP

PIPEX Ltd.
216 Cambridge Science Park
Cambridge, CB4 4WA

The Direct Connection
P O Box 931
London, SE18 3PW

INDEX